W9-BCL-176

WENHAM
MASS. 01984

DISCARDED
JENKS LRC
GORDON COLLEGE

OCEAN WANDERERS

WANDERERS

*The Migratory Sea Birds
of the World*

onald Mathais

R. M. LOCKLEY

*With drawings by Robert Gillmor,
9 colour plates, 28 black and
white photographs and 22 maps*

DAVID & CHARLES Newton Abbot London Vancouver
STACKPOLE BOOKS *Harrisburg*

This edition first published in 1974
in Great Britain by
David & Charles (Holdings) Limited Newton Abbot Devon
in the United States in 1973 by
Stackpole Books Harrisburg Pa

ISBN 0 7153 5713 1 (*Great Britain*)
ISBN 0 8117 1133 1 (*United States*)

© R. M. Lockley 1974
All rights reserved. No part of this
publication may be reproduced, stored
in a retrieval system, or transmitted,
in any form or by any means, electronic,
mechanical, photocopying, recording or
otherwise, without the prior permission
of the publisher.

QL
673
.L7
1974

Set in 11 on 13pt Bembo and printed in
Great Britain by Ebenezer Baylis & Son Limited Worcester
for David & Charles (Holdings) Limited
South Devon House Newton Abbot Devon

Published in Canada by Douglas David &
Charles Limited 3645 McKechnie Drive
West Vancouver BC

CONTENTS

ACKNOWLEDGEMENTS

My warmest thanks to all those, named and unnamed, who have directly and indirectly assisted in the making of this book. Some have worked in the field with me, at sea, and ashore on small islands, especially in those early days when so little was known of the life histories of the petrels, auks and gulls. To them and to the increasing body of younger observers who are contributing important new studies of the lives of the ocean wanderers, my thanks again, my apologies for these limited acknowledgements, and for any sins of omission.

LIST OF ILLUSTRATIONS

FIGURES

INTRODUCTION

This book describes the lives of those specialised flying machines, the birds which wander restlessly yet with purpose over the great oceans of the world, and as far as possible avoid the land: ranging from the beautiful, noble albatrosses—giant sailplaners of storm latitudes—to the least and smallest of the ocean wanderers, the fragile-looking storm petrels which walk on the surface of the sea, and the dainty, elegant phalaropes: both fly thousands of miles across the equator, and ride out the gales with no less success.

All these birds must nest on stable ground, but at other times when far from land most of them use the sea as their resting and sleeping cradle. But not all: a few are never seen to alight voluntarily on water, although they snatch their food from the surface in swooping or hovering flight. Some of these may fly continuously, when far from land, for whole days and nights, perhaps not sleeping (as we know sleep) for weeks, even months. If so, this is an adaptation obviously valuable for survival in storm latitudes and during persistent high winds and gales. But the sea bird has solved other formidable problems of ocean existence.

For example, living for days and weeks in the open sea, man would die if he was forced to depend on salt water to quench his thirst, as he must do to replace evaporated body water. Although it is possible for him to survive for a while if he drinks only small quantities of salt water, eventually his internal salt balance is deranged beyond recovery. Wholly marine birds have no access to fresh water; they have overcome the problem by discharging excess salt, in the form of sodium chloride at high concentrations, through special nasal glands.

Perhaps the most intriguing problem arising from the study of ocean wanderers, from sea birds to fish, turtles and whales, is that of their marvellous sense of geographical position on the face of the globe, which enables them to orientate and navigate accurately across hundreds or thousands of miles of ocean, featureless to man, between their summer breeding grounds and their wintering or non-breeding sea quarters. How do they do it?

Another remarkable skill is the ability of the young inexperienced sea bird, in those species deserted by the parents before it leaves the nest, to make the same long migration over the empty sea, totally without adult guidance.

To begin to understand these adaptations to ocean-going we need to examine how sea birds came to migrate in the first place, why some travel thousands, some hundreds, of miles, and others not at all; what prompts and controls the times and distances of these voyages, and their directions—transequatorially from one hemisphere to another, a few latitudinally around the southern oceans, and one almost from pole to pole. Inevitably we find ourselves asking more fundamental questions, such as why sea birds exist at all; why there are so many, or so few, in certain ocean zones; and what special factors regulate their increase or decrease, or stabilise their numbers?

As a young man I lived for several years continuously, and in other years intermittently, on small islands used as breeding grounds by some of these oceanic birds. In making an original study of the breeding habits of shearwater, storm petrel, puffin and other species I was fascinated by many aspects of their behaviour which could not be explained except theoretically. Other studies by later observers on the same islands, and at sea-bird colonies in remote places in all oceans, have greatly added to our knowledge of their habits, as described in this book. But further problems of sea-bird behaviour remain unsolved.

I have tried here to present what we know and what we do not know about the life histories of oceanic birds, and their relations with man. Handbooks to the identification of the 300 or so species and subspecies of sea birds of all oceans of the world are already available (see bibliography). After describing the evolution and speciation of sea birds over the world, my aim is to enable the reader to understand something of their very remarkable adaptations to ocean-going, their breeding ecology, and their interlocking migrations, even as he admires their graceful forms and skill in air and water. My hope too is that by such understanding he may appreciate, and actively help, the work of those who are pressing for world protection of the rarer ocean wanderers, and for the provision of more sanctuaries at their nesting grounds, the majority of which are no longer inaccessible, but are in danger of adverse exploitation.

1 ORIGIN AND EVOLUTION

The world of birds is one of marvellous contrasts. We may wonder at the disparity between the tiny stay-at-home wren, content to fly and feed and nest within a a few square yards of a sheltered garden, and the giant albatross which glides with ease thousands of miles on the gales of the 'roaring forties' latitude of the southern oceans. There are even some birds which cannot fly at all; most of these live sedentary terrestrial lives or migrate only short distances on foot. But some flightless sea birds, notably penguins, may swim far, we do not yet know how far, on seasonal journeys.

Birds, like all living organisms, need food, and this need has played the major part in their diversification—each species becoming specialised for the exploitation of a particular food source. Hence each comes to occupy its own ecological niche within the environment, in which it lives and multiplies and outside which it cannot survive.

To trace the way in which the winged wanderers of today have evolved by exploiting the available sea-food supply will take us far back to the newly created world of thousands of millions of years ago.

Probably life began in the sea. In the warmth of Earth's first oceans, hydrogen, carbon and other elements and compounds mixed and separated and recombined in ever-changing forms. Over millions of slowly cooling epochs organic life was evolving from new compounds floating in the tropical sea. At last the protozoan cell appeared—living tissue wrapped in a tough but permeable membrane through which it assimilated nourishment from the environment. Plant life came first: energy from sunlight combined with chlorophyll and the elements of air and water to produce sugar and starch, and new multicellular structures arose.

Perhaps 1,000 million years ago the first, unicellular, animal life was born; larger and more complex forms followed—sponges, worms, molluscs and arthropods, many of which floated in the upper layers of ocean to form the plankton, the basis of the marine food chain on which the sea birds of today depend.

The first vertebrates appeared some 500 million years ago during the Ordovician period—primitive fish-like creatures which gave rise to the true fishes which flourished in succeeding eras. Amphibians proliferated during the Carboniferous period and gave rise to the reptiles, better adapted to a terrestrial existence, which quickly became the dominant form of vertebrate life, exploiting the seas, freshwater swamps, dry land and, with the evolution of the pterosaurs, exploring the possibilities of aerial life.

The birds derive from a group of small bipedal dinosaurs, and the earliest known example is the Jurassic *Archaeopteryx*, which appeared about 150 million years ago. It could climb and glide; but it could not fly.

EVOLUTION

Slowly but surely new birds evolved, capable of sustained flight and manoeuvring in the air over land and sea, and thus able to seek and find unoccupied niches of living space and food supply. The species of animal and plant life on which these birds fed were likewise diversifying during further millions of years of evolution.

The rate of radiation into new genera and families intensified about 35 million years ago (the Oligocene epoch of the Tertiary era), when many fossils of now extinct, often very large, birds were laid down. Of sea birds, albatrosses, shearwaters and petrels speciated during this period; and the present families of penguins, gannets, boobies and auks were established. Possibly some smaller species are almost as old, such as the sea-wandering phalaropes of the wader family, but the fragile bones of little birds seldom appear in the fossil record—in life they were devoured and digested by predators, as they are today. The phalaropes belong to the large order of the Charadriiformes, which developed into many families possibly as late as 10 million years ago, and include the terns, gulls, skuas and waders.

Today some 270 true species of sea birds survive whose development has been aquatic, if not wholly marine. Some have become more pelagic (ocean-dwelling) and others more terrestrial even to the extent of breeding, and in a few instances living, far inland by lake and river (certain gulls and terns). This book is concerned only with those which have remained or become oceanic and wandering.

As no bird has so far succeeded in incubating its egg afloat on the sea, like the mythical halcyon, we may next consider where the first birds did nest and rear their young, and from that early birthplace colonise all oceans of the world.

In the days of the archaeopteryx the configuration of the world land masses was very different from their topography today. At one remote period the present ice-covered Antarctica was a pleasant sunlit land, watered by abundant mild rain, rich with plant life; it is believed to have been the southern part of the mysterious undefined Gondwanaland—the land of undivided continents of the geomorphologist—which was possibly completely or nearly joined, 100 million years ago

Common terns, with the comparatively slow, steady beating of their wings, can fly steadily for hours, perhaps days, at a time

in the Jurassic and early Cretaceous periods, to other southern land masses and great islands, of which South America, Australia and New Zealand are the southernmost temperate portions surviving today. Proof of a more genial climate is given by recent recoveries of numerous plant and animal fossils on the present south polar continent. Although its interior is now covered with an immense ice-cap thousands of metres thick at the South Pole, echo-sounding and core tests indicate that the antarctic 'continent' may yet prove to be an archipelago, parts of its land mass sunk below existing sea level, perhaps still sinking under the enormous weight of ice. In the Tertiary period the drifting shores of Gondwanaland would have been inhabited by early forms of sea birds—certainly giant primitive forms of penguins. During this warm period, lasting between 100 million and 1 million years BP (Before Present), world sea level was higher than it is now, since little or none of earth's fresh water, derived in the first place from the ocean, was locked in polar ice-caps and mountain glaciers. A hotter sun evaporated the surface waters of a much wider tropical sea, and this atmospheric moisture fell as heavy rain upon the few drifting land masses above sea level.

About a million years ago (the Pleistocene) there was a dramatic change in the earth's surface as the planet cooled off following a convulsive period of volcanic activity, mountain building, ocean-floor spreading, and division of Gondwanaland from the northern land masses. Sea level fell by as much as 300m, as ice-caps built up at the poles and on the high ground of temperate latitudes. The continents settled down more or less as we know them today; and the early forms of sea birds—what happened to them?

Representatives of all the modern families were already well established and occupying the new major oceans, but the reshaped continents and cooling world climate, resembling that of the present day, had caused changes in the circulation of sea currents which affected their food supply, as discussed later in this book.

Next came the four glaciations of the last 100,000 years, each causing a fall of ocean level, followed by a rise during warmer interglacial intervals. On the slow approach of each glaciation Antarctica—now drifted to its present isolated position—became covered with a thick snow-fed ice-cap, and the less mobile species of plants and animals were frozen out. But sea birds and seals had ample time to fly or swim north across the shrinking ocean, to find food in warmer seas and new coasts and islands on which to breed. When the most recent climatic amelioration set in, some 10,000 years ago, with ocean levels rising again as polar ice and glaciers melted, there would be some return to the south, to establish the breeding and feeding grounds in high latitudes as we know them today. For as we shall see the chilly waters around the polar ice-cap are extremely rich in sea foods.

Similarly, in the north these glacial periods brought the north polar ice-sheet south, almost to latitude $50°N$, with the same effect: birds and other mobile species established above that latitude were forced to move south in search of food and breeding quarters—or perish. But as far as we know there has never, in the history of life on earth, been an arctic land-mass uncovered by ice much beyond $85°N$ (the present approximate limits of the Arctic Ocean), and there is very little ocean between $80°N$ and $60°N$—an area occupied chiefly by the cool continental block of North America and northern Eurasia. So the numbers of sea birds are fewer than in those same latitudes south, which are wide open with the largest expanse of salt water in the world, surrounding Antarctica.

SEA-BIRD NUMBERS

The oceans cover rather less than three-quarters of the earth's surface. The oceanic surface of the southern hemisphere occupies roughly two-thirds of this expanse of salt water. It is not surprising therefore more species of oceanic birds originated from a predominately southern source—as the fossil record bears evidence. The world's living species of primary marine birds are distributed as follows:

South Pacific	128	North Pacific	107
South Atlantic	73	North Atlantic	74
Indian Ocean	73	Mediterranean	24
Antarctic	44	Arctic	31
Total	318	*Total*	236

(The list includes species which wander both sides of the equator, although they may breed only in one hemisphere.)

Approximately one-quarter more species are found in southern oceans. But these figures of course are for species only, and do not prove that greater numbers of individual oceanic birds per square mile or kilometre exist in the south, although this is likely to be so. Obviously the penguin family had its source in the far south: except for the isolated Galapagos penguin, which even though it breeds at the equator feeds in the cool Humboldt Current southwards, penguins are confined to the southern hemisphere. The majority of the vast order of the tube-nosed birds (albatrosses, shearwaters and petrels) inhabit southern oceans. But as we shall see,

Great shearwater in flight

evidently a few families such as the gulls and auks enjoyed their greatest speciation and adaptive radiation north of the equator.

Systematists have divided animals into groups known as orders and families according to their physiological structure and morphological (size, shape, colour) characters. On this classification the oceanic species of birds are divided into some 270 species:

Order	Family	No of Species
Sphenisciformes	Spheniscidae: Penguins	15
Procellariiformes	Diomedeidae: Albatrosses	13
	Procellariidae: Fulmars, Petrels, Shearwaters	60
	Hydrobatidae: Storm Petrels	18
	Pelecanoididae: Diving Petrels	5
Pelecaniformes:	Phaethontidae: Tropic Birds	3
	Pelecanidae: Pelicans	1
	Sulidae: Gannets, Boobies	9
	Phalacrocoracidae: Cormorants	35
	Anhingidae: Darters	(1)
	Fregatidae: Frigate Birds	5
Charadriiformes	Chionididae: Sheathbills	2
	Stercorariidae: Skuas	4
	Laridae: Gulls	42
	Sternidae: Terns, Noddies	39
	Rynchidae: Skimmers	3
	Alcidae: Auks	22
	Phalalaropodidae: Phalaropes	2

We have already remarked that some sea birds are not ocean wanderers. Several gulls and terns, the darters and skimmers, visit the sea briefly. Nor have I included a number of wading birds which nest along coasts and inland, but make considerable transocean crossings on their winter migration. They are listed in the last chapter.

Watching the millions of muttonbird shearwaters in and around the Bass Strait between Australia and Tasmania, the observer could justifiably conclude that there could be no greater assemblage of birds in 20 miles of seaway elsewhere in the world—until he has seen the dense flights of little auks at rookeries in the high Arctic, or tried to estimate the millions of guanay cormorants, boobies and pelicans coming and going to and from the Bird Islands of Peru. Can the world population of these and other abundant birds be counted with any degree of accuracy? Hardly. There have been, however, censuses of breeding species in given localities which are at least of historical interest. When James Fisher and I were writing a book on North Atlantic sea birds, we collected world data on the numbers of thirty-six species (Fisher & Lockley, 1954). With the deepening interest in the conservation and economic importance of sea birds, and with modern transport providing easier access, observers are paying more attention to assessing their populations, particularly through study groups now established in Europe, America, and Australasia. Where available, recent census figures are given in the chapters dealing with the species concerned in such counts and estimates.

Sooty shearwaters, or muttonbirds, which migrate from the breeding grounds in the far south to 'winter' in the northern hemisphere summer

SPECIATION—THE ISOLATING MECHANISM

The evolution of species is a natural continuing process: species are born even as other species become extinct. The individual does not change, even though it

(*Facing page*) Black-browed albatross at sea

differs from its sibling. As in man, the bird exhibits this individual variability within the general pattern of its specific genetic structure and behaviour. Darwin concluded that both inherited characters and acquired variations could be transmitted to the progeny, and so produce new species by natural selection of the most advantageous physiological and behavioural changes in the individual. We now know that natural selection operates through inherited factors only, by the combination of the genes and chromosomes in the germ plasm in those species which reproduce sexually. The evolutionary unit is the group rather than the individual. Species have been redefined: they are groups of actually or potentially interbreeding natural populations, which are reproductively isolated from other such groups (Mayr, 1942).

The infinite number of combinations and exchanges of heritable characters which take place on fertilisation of the ovum by the sperm ensure uniformity in the species, but at the same time produce the slight differences we note in individuals therein. To us, birds of one species often seem identical, but to each other they are recognisable as quite distinct individuals. Only occasionally is there a rare genetic combination (possibly at times a spontaneous change within the gene itself) resulting in alteration (mutation) in the genes which has beneficial survival value for the group. Most mutations are disadvantageous and often lethal: in birds these include albinism, taillessness, twisted feet, inverted, incomplete or excessive feathering. Some of these freaks have been used by man to establish new domestic varieties of fowls and pigeons, fixing the aberrant characters by selective inbreeding on Mendelian principles.

In nature it is only the useful (adaptive) mutations which survive to provide the raw material for evolutionary change. But this only occurs when the mutation becomes established in a sufficient number of individuals interbreeding in isolation from the parent stock. Reproductive isolation is the hallmark of speciation, and species arise therein by a definable process.

Geographic separation is a primary stimulus, as when a group breaks away from the centre and colonises elsewhere, so interrupting the exchange of genes which hitherto maintained the common heredity. In a sense to break away spontaneously is a mutation in itself, because it is a deviation from normal behaviour. (The gene for colonising, wandering or migrating can become dominant in a hitherto sedentary species, it is thought; for example, in the northern Atlantic race of the fulmar, which in the last half-century has colonised vigorously southward.) Once established in new territory, further changes in the genetic composition of the group, together with environmental influences of food, climate and terrain, in centuries of time, produce the new race, species or genus.

Clear examples of speciation in geographic isolation in sea birds are seen in the skuas; the great skua, wandering from nesting islands in the far North Atlantic, has settled to breed and subspeciate in the far south, where it is numerically more abundant, and enjoys a wider breeding range. Conversely it is likely that the antarctic fulmars nesting in the far south are the parent stock from which individuals reached the northern hemisphere, and speciated into two distinct races, if not species, breeding in high latitudes in the Pacific and the Arctic, and living at all times in those chill waters. The most northerly breeding tern in the world, the arctic sea-swallow, migrates to 'winter' in the summer of Antarctica, where its sedentary offshoot, the antarctic tern, is regarded as a true species—it is reproductively isolated, but in breeding plumage it is difficult to distinguish from the arctic tern,

(*Facing page*) Manx shearwaters at burrow on a wet night, Skomer Island

which however has assumed a drab winter plumage and moults during its sojourn south (see page 145).

(see page 145)

How far back in time these instances of speciation in geographic isolation occurred is uncertain; but adaptive radiation of marine species was clearly speeded up by the physical separation of the oceans during the land-building period of the late Pliocene and early Pleistocene, over a million years ago. The Isthmus of Panama emerged to make a land bridge joining the two Americas, permitting the exchange of terrestrial fauna but reproductively isolating the salt-water dwellers. This allowed the present distinct marine faunas of the tropical and sub-tropical Pacific, and of the Caribbean coasts of America, to develop and diverge. In sea birds this barrier has produced separate but closely allied species of boobies, shearwaters, petrels, cormorants and pelicans.

Where geographical isolation is incomplete, as in species breeding over a wide, more or less unbroken, range of coasts and islands, there are nevertheless often visible differences in appearance (chiefly colour and size) becoming progressively stronger outward from the original centre of population, producing what Julian Huxley has named a cline—a gradual variation of characters with distribution. A colour cline appears through the geographic races of man; his skin colour is an adaptive mutation to climatic factors: black in the tropics, pale in temperate zones. But the races of man, although they are often hostile towards each other, are not yet even subspecies, since they interbreed freely.

Long-tailed skua, a trans-equatorial migrant which breeds in the high Arctic

＊ The gulls are excellent examples of colour clines and races approaching sub-specific rank, and reaching true speciation. The herring gull *Larus argentatus* can be divided into a chain of some twelve distinct races or related species breeding over all temperate coasts and inland seas north of the equator. They are not pelagic, and tend to breed selectively in groups according to food and habitat preferences, but where the breeding grounds of two members of this chain overlap they will inter-breed. For example the pale-mantled herring gull will mate with the dark-mantled lesser black-backed *L. fuscus*, of the same size, but neither will mate (or very rarely) with the larger great black-backed gull *L. marinus*, nesting in the same colony. Mating between *argentatus* and *fuscus* is fertile, but not frequent enough to result in a merger. Although the two coexist (are 'sympatric') there are differences in their ecology which make this possible. The herring gull has slightly different feeding habits and prefers to nest in an open situation (cliff, scree, dune); the lesser black-back selects low plant cover. They live together, but are ecologically isolated. Moreover the herring gull is sedentary, the other is migratory, flying coastwise and overland hundreds of miles southward in winter. Indeed the lesser black-backed gull must at one time have wandered exceptionally across the equator and occupied a vacant niche in the temperate latitudes of southern coasts, where it is widespread, highly successful and increasing. It has retained the voice, display, colour of plumage, and nesting behaviour of *L. fuscus*. But because it has become slightly larger it has earned the specific name of *L. dominicanus* (dominican, kelp or southern black-backed gull are common names); it has also become more aggressive towards other species, in fact occupying in the southern hemisphere the niche which the bullying, predatory *L. marinus* has in the north—another fascinating example of a group from a migratory species, coexisting in ecological isolation with a related species, transferring to live and speciate in geographic isolation, where it has become sedentary.

It was an advantage for the new *L. dominicanus* to become aggressive and larger, thereby dominating all other gulls coexisting in its present geographical range: southern South America, South Africa, the sub-antarctic islands and New Zealand. It had not colonised Australia until recently, probably because the temperate coasts there were pre-occupied by the powerful Pacific gull *L. pacificus*, the southern hemisphere counterpart of the northern *L. marinus*, which *pacificus* closely resembles in habits, size, dark mantle and voice, although it has a larger bill and black-tipped tail. Despite its larger size *pacificus* is losing ground geographically and numerically: at least *dominicanus* is taking over breeding sites along the Australian coast vacated by the Pacific gull.

No two species can coexist in nature unless their ecology differs. Where one species invades the breeding and feeding grounds of another, the competition for identical food and nesting space eliminates the weaker. In the northern chain (superspecies or species-group) of *L. argentatus* gulls referred to above, although we have seen that coexisting subspecies or races of like size will interbreed, those geographically separated by several links in the chain will have no opportunity to do so—since they do not meet at the nesting grounds. At the ends of the chain however, if two members do coincide on a common breeding ground, they do not mate (or are intersterile if they do) but are able to coexist because their genetic characters have progressively changed, altering colour, size, habits and ecology. Although both are sprung from the same parent stock, they have diverged in different directions, and become so different from each other that they behave in that respect as distinct species—an example of 'speciation by distance'. A similar speciation in northern albatrosses is discussed on page 99.

It was Julian Huxley who pioneered the idea that size differences between congeneric birds will produce ecological isolation; the larger individuals may dominate the competition for food and nesting sites in a colony of the same or related species. If they survive to reproduce successfully, the smaller weaker birds will have adapted to the position in various ways, such as breeding at a different time of year, poorer or different nesting sites, and smaller or otherwise different food species (many birds, eg gulls, terns, petrels, with now distinct large, medium and small races or subspecies of one 'superspecies'). They will have created, by genetic selection of the fittest to survive in the new environment, their own ecological isolation, and opportunity to diverge and evolve as a full species.

The superspecies *Puffinus* shearwater offers an intriguing example of current evolution by adaptive mutation of large, small and medium races, subspecies and species in all oceans of the world, as described in the chapter on shearwaters. To take the case of the medium-sized *Puffinus puffinus*, which has several Atlantic, Mediterranean, Pacific and Indian Ocean representatives, the one breeding in northwestern Europe is the type species Manx shearwater *P. puffinus*, which nests in burrows on suboceanic islands, sea-cliffs and mountain tops. Proposals by taxonomists to separate into two subspecies the island-cliff breeders from those breeding on cold mountain tops at over 2,000ft in the Hebrides, and around 5,000ft in Madeira, have not been scientifically acceptable. They may be topographically isolated by their selection of breeding sites (and so far marking studies have not proved an interchange of population which would destroy genetical isolation), but in the hand they are indistinguishable. The Manx shearwater migrates in winter

Giant petrel or stinker, a rapacious carrion-eater as large as a small albatross

to the South Atlantic, and it seems that there is sufficient exchange of individuals (perhaps initially at sea) over the whole breeding range to prevent subspeciation therein.

The Manx shearwater is a great ocean-goer but apparently has rarely wandered into the Pacific, which was probably its prehistoric home ocean. One individual marked at Skokholm in Wales was, however, washed up dead in SE Australia, and another (unmarked) in the North Island of New Zealand. These isolated records could have been fortuitous, ship-aided accidents; yet, as this bird is such a powerful flier, normally covering at least 12,000 miles on its transatlantic migration annually, small groups could be irregular visitors in any of the world's oceans, either when storm-driven or during the idle years of adolescence before returning home to breed for the first time. In that case these wanderers, 'lost' in an alien ocean, would be potential material for evolution into new species in geographic isolation if they established a breeding unit on finding suitable unoccupied territory and an agreeable food supply. But what are their chances?

It has already been suggested that it was through similar wandering or 'lost' groups of individuals that the fulmar petrel colonised the Arctic from the original southern stock, and by a similar abmigration the lesser black-backed gull of Europe became the kelp gull of the southern hemisphere. These random successful colonisations were probably part of the rapid speciation following the birth of new islands and continents over a million years ago, which provided vast areas of new coastal breeding sites. Although, as we have seen in the instances of the Atlantic fulmar, the kelp and Pacific gulls, there are detectable local and regional shifts of population and species in the present century, long-distance colonisation of wintering quarters in high latitudes by species hitherto breeding exclusively in high latitudes in the other hemisphere is rare today, and when it occurs may be impermanent. The European swallow has begun to breed in its South African winter range; but there seem to be no records in historic times of an oceanic bird making a similar transequatorial transfer of a breeding group over vast distances. Albatrosses have wandered as far north as Spitzbergen on an abnormal migration, and have joined a gannet colony in the Faeroe Islands, remaining there for years, but without breeding (page 99).

The most formidable of the difficulties facing the Manx shearwater (to continue with a species I have studied over several decades) attempting to breed in the southern hemisphere would be its failure to achieve geological or ecological isolation: the *suitable* breeding sites—islands, cliffs and mountain tops—are already occupied by the resident *Puffinus* representatives, so much more abundant in southern seas. In New Zealand there are two close relatives (considered by some to be only races) of *P. puffinus*, which would offer competitive exclusion; also, if by chance a Manx shearwater pair succeeded in nesting within the breeding ground of either, the progeny, 'knowing' only New Zealand and its seas, might nevertheless have to resist the innate programming for navigation (discussed in Chapter 5) which the normal fledgling carries out, unaided by its parents, in the Atlantic. Having overcome this formidable genetic pressure by remaining in southern Pacific waters (as migratory Atlantic salmon have when hatched from ova transplanted from Europe and deposited in Australasian rivers), and having survived the usual period of adolescence at sea where they would be competing with the local *Puffinus* races for the same organisms in the sea food chain, the second and subsequent generations would disappear as a separate race by interbreeding with the long-established *Puffinus*.

At sea the Manx shearwater *P. puffinus* is virtually indistinguishable from the New Zealand *P. gavia*, the fluttering shearwater, or from the other local medium-sized shearwater, *P. huttoni*. In the hand the three show only slight differences in plumage colour and marking, but measurements overlap. Hence it is hardly surprising that taxonomists have lumped them together as one species. *Gavia* nests abundantly on small offshore islands, but the nesting place of *huttoni*, which feeds in the same waters (Tasman Sea and Cook Strait) as *gavia*, was unknown until 1965, when it was discovered breeding in the barren crags of the Seaward Kaikoura Mountain of South Island, New Zealand, more than 4,000ft (1,213m) above sea level. Here then, was the parallel in New Zealand of the Manx shearwaters breeding in separate topographical sites of island and mountain top in Europe. Indeed, there is the very remote possibility (virtually impossible to prove except perhaps by extensive physiological and histological comparison and serum tests for affinities) that *huttoni* is derived from abmigrated *puffinus* from Europe; but the reverse is more likely. What is now clear is that *huttoni*, whether derived from *puffinus* or *gavia*, has earned specific rank by breeding in both geographic and ecological isolation. The former is provided by mountain-breeding, the latter by its distinct ecology: *huttoni*, influenced by the chill climate of the Kaikoura heights, which are snow-covered until late in spring, breeds at least two months later than *gavia*. Other distinguishing characters are the slightly longer bill, suggesting a difference in feeding—probably it selects smaller or larger organisms in the food chain; slightly larger size (to resist mountain cold—conforming to Bergmann's rule that because there is less heat-loss per unit of weight, cold-climate breeders are larger than their more tropical relatives?); and its migration farther west along the south coast of Australia than *gavia*, which remains in the Tasman Sea east of Australia.

ECOLOGICAL NICHES

In later chapters describing the life histories of oceanic birds, further examples of the principle of ecological isolation by which related and unrelated species coexist without serious threat to one another's existence, will be apparent. There is a very fine balance in this sharing and use of environmental factors (the ecosystem); it is fascinating to try to assess it by studying the adaptive devices and behaviour of the species involved. As discussed in the next chapter the differences can be slight or obvious: for example on close examination, where related species from a mixed nesting colony feed on the same fish or other marine organisms, altogether at sea, it will be found that each species takes the prey at different depths and by different pursuit and capture methods, in this way perhaps selecting different age and size levels in the same prey. The varied bill structure in closely related species (eg auks), is a more obvious indication of different feeding methods.

The endless adaptive devices for survival are astonishing and exciting: the variants can be classified under three main, interdependent, headings.

Physiological: structure and function of living tissue, especially of the brain, muscles, respiratory, locomotive and reproductive organs.

Morphological: differences of size, shape and colour.

Behavioural: relating to feeding, courtship and reproductive actions, migration.

2 ADAPTATIONS TO OCEAN-GOING

Sea birds have dispersed and speciated over the oceans of the world largely by flying, only a few by swimming. All sea birds can swim, for which purpose their webbed feet are specially adapted. A few (terns and tropic birds) prefer to swim as little as possible, and some (frigate birds) not at all, even when hundreds of miles from land. Penguins are flightless, but nevertheless some travel long distances on migration, and one has colonised north to the equator, dropping off one group (which has become the Peruvian *Spheniscus humboldti*) on the way. This most northerly breeding penguin is the Galapagos *S. mendiculus*; and in the Galapagos Islands it coexists with another flightless bird of the sea, the Galapagos cormorant. Presumably this cormorant was able to fly, long ago, before its progenitor reached the safety of isolation from man and every other mammalian predator, and settled down to a peaceful island existence, its wings superfluous and degenerated, by genetic mutation, to functionless feathered relics. Its large webbed feet provide its sole method of locomotion on land and in the sea.

FLIGHT

The archaeopteryx could glide, but could not fly properly; but by modifying the forelimbs still further its descendants became specialised flying machines of great diversity. Penguins adapted to flight under water, albatrosses became the first long-distance sailplaners, falcons and swifts the fastest fliers, kestrels and sea-swallows

25

(terns) expert at vertical flight, hovering, rising and falling like helicopters, and small woodland birds developed broad complex wings with emarginated edges and slots which gave extreme manoeuvrability and control for movement in any direction through thick foliage. In sea birds, which have the whole ocean to move about in, the warbler's agility is unnecessary, but the frigate bird, with its long wings and tail, is a master of aerial twists and turns, mid-air stops and starts, as it snatches up its moving prey—flying fish or the food vomited from the crop of another bird in flight.

Aircraft designers have copied the general shape of the bird wing, convex above and concave below, thick and strongest at the forward edge containing bone and muscles, thin and flexible at the trailing edge—the tips of the quill feathers. This aerofoil shape produces the lift force (upward air flow) when the wing moves forward with the leading edge higher than the trailing edge. The wider this angle of attack relative to the horizontal the greater the lift; until the point is reached, before the wing is vertical, when the upward flow of air ceases and becomes turbulent. This results in stalling, used by the bird as a brake for landing—and in hovering. At stalling point, the bird counters the force of gravity to prevent crashing to the ground by wing-beating in the stalled position, and manipulation of the muscles to spread wide the flexible feathers of the wings and tail. Birds with medium broad wings (gulls and terns) land gently and with ease, but it is difficult for the long-winged albatrosses and shearwaters to land gracefully; like fast aircraft they must taxi along the ground head to wind for some distance before being able to stop, or water-ski with webbed feet, braked wings and spread tail, unless there is a strong headwind to reduce surface speed; and conversely on take-off.

Calculations of flight performances of birds in terms of modern aerodynamics are complicated by too many variables. However certain measurements applied to aircraft can be used as a rough guide: these are wing-loading (weight divided by wing area); aspect ratio (wing span divided by average 'chord' or width of wing); and gliding angle (weight divided by span). The weight of a bird's engines—that is, its wing muscles—does give some indication of its flight potentiality when expressed as a percentage of total body weight. This is the power-weight ratio. Both power-weight and aspect ratio are high in soaring and gliding birds with long wings and weak muscles, and low in birds, such as pheasant, pigeon and humming bird, with broad muscular wings suited to fast flapping and vertical take-off.

The dynamic soaring and gliding of albatrosses is discussed in Chapter 8. Soaring with little or no flapping of the fully spread wings is only possible if the air is rising faster than the rate of sink (gravity). Sea birds take advantage of thermal columns of warm air rising above sun-heated surfaces of islands, sands and calm seas. They also soar in currents caused by wind deflected upwards against cliffs, ships and the sea wave itself. Continuous fast gliding is difficult for small lightweight birds, most of which beat their wings continuously to maintain height. Large, proportionately heavy birds with short broad wings can glide only for short distances (auks, herons, swans, ducks, pheasants) and seldom or never soar. Only large long-winged birds (the larger petrels especially, and vultures) can sustain long periods of fast sailplaning. Although weight causes gravitational drag, at speed it gives greater penetration (compare velocity of the cannon ball with that of a feather, launched with equal force), and the long-winged glider controls its rapid flight by altering

Royal albatross — ocean wanderer of the southern hemisphere

the camber of the wing, by slightly closing the wing-tips to reduce air resistance and increase ground speed, or fully spreading the wings to reduce speed and increase lift.

The degree of friction and turbulence caused by air flow may possibly be controlled secondarily by muscular raising and flattening of plumage surfaces, often seen in birds, especially in display and preening activities. Swimming penguins, seals and dolphins, it is said, can reduce the turbulence of water along their sleek bodies by muscular control of the surface of the skin.

Flapping flight is complex, especially in small birds such as auks, which beat their wings rapidly. Owing to the extreme flexibility of the wing feathers, the air, grasped by the initial forward-downward stroke of the leading edge, is filtered through the widely spread quills at the trailing edge, which bends upwards, before the completion of the propulsion stroke. On the upstroke the wing folds towards the body in a *backward* movement, and the primaries twist and open like venetian blinds, both movements reducing air resistance to a minimum. In effect the wings are twin variable pitch propellors rather than rigid paddles.

The action in larger birds (gulls, terns, gannets), which flap their wings slowly by comparison, and do not fold them so much, is a compromise between whirring and gliding flight; the long wing is seen to demonstrate two main functions: the arm, forming the inner wing with its trailing edge of secondary flight feathers, is held almost rigid and horizontal from shoulder through elbow to wrist, turning but slightly at the fulcrum of the shoulder girdle; it acts as a stabiliser and provides lift. Motive power is provided by the muscles which alternately pull down and lift up the outer wing (the hand) at the hinge of the wrist. The highly flexible wing-tips—the primary flight feathers—circle through the air in an arc of up to 180°, providing the forward drive on the downstroke, but decelerating slightly on the upstroke, when thrust is lost. The action is more like that of a paddle thrusting in and slipping out of the water.

Pelicans, gannets and many other large birds frequently fly in close formation, flapping when the leader flaps, and gliding when it glides. The line-ahead formation is most economical of energy, each bird taking advantage of the cushion of turbulent air rising in the wake of the bird in front. Chevron formation is less efficient, as only the swirling air behind one wing of the bird in front is available; but this V-shaped formation gives each bird a clearer view ahead. At intervals a fresh bird will replace the leader when the latter is tired and falls behind.

FEATHER CARE

The temperature of a bird's body is higher than in man: 106°F (41°C) by day, dropping a few degrees F at night. These temperatures are secured by the insulation of the skin with a cushion of body-warmed air imprisoned by the overlapping feathers of the plumage, which is rendered waterproof by regular preening and oiling. With its bill the bird squeezes droplets of fatty oil from the nodule of the uropygial (preen) gland above the tail, and conveys these to every feather in turn in nibbling, wiping and stropping actions, fluffing out its plumage to give access to underlying feathers and down. It rubs the back of the head against the gland, and so transfers the oil to parts of the body inaccessible to the bill; and the foot, rubbed with the oily head or beak, is likewise lubricated against water and weather.

Sea birds at rest spend hours systematically working through their plumage. Loosened feathers are removed during the moult, and dropped. But dust, fine feather scale, lice, and weathered preen oil—which produces vitamin D upon irradiation in sunlight—are invariably swallowed, and are probably an important contribution to health, both nutritionally and by control of parasites.

In animals the comfort movements of preening, scratching, licking, and rubbing of the body against objects are an instinctive reaction to local irritation of the sensitive skin. The effect is functional, stimulative; and often infectious (easily copied) in a flock of birds, as yawning and itching is in human society. Siblings in the nest will copy the example of their parents and preen each other; but if the stronger nestling breaks the tender skin of the weaker, it may if hungry, proceed to devour it piece-meal (skuas, some gulls and raptors). Mutual preening in paired birds is described below: it is largely a substitute activity.

Bathing is also part of feather care. Even birds which spend most of their days swimming and diving are observed to bathe regularly. The body and tail feathers are ruffled open to allow penetration by water, which at the same time is thrown over the back by a scooping action of the head and neck, and by beating and whirling the wings to create a fountain of spray towards the body. However, although water reaches the skin to wash away loose debris and parasites, this, like the feathers, is protected by its greasy surface from becoming saturated. Insulation and warmth are vigorously restored by raising and jerking the body, and flapping of wings clear of the water, thus centrifugally expelling the water from the contour feathers—now depressed for the purpose.

SURPLUS SALT EXCRETION

In drinking sea water voluntarily, and taking it incidentally when feeding and in preening its feathers, the sea bird absorbs far more salt than it needs for health, or can dispose of through the normal renal excretory system. In the form of highly concentrated sodium chloride (with some potassium) the surplus salt is rapidly conveyed by a network of blood vessels into fine tubes connected with the nasal glands, which discharge it externally. After feeding in and drinking salt water, sea birds will nose-drip these chemicals in solution; or in certain diving birds (gannets, cormorants) in which the nostrils are blocked externally (to prevent water being forced into the lungs on impact with the sea) the solution trickles from the nasal entrance situated in the roof of the mouth, and out of the mouth when these birds are not diving. As birds do not normally sneeze, the secretion is dispersed by vigorous head-shaking.

OIL SECRETION AND EXCRETION

In addition to their large tail glands which yield oil for preening, all members of the petrel family, from the mighty albatross to the sparrow-sized storm petrel, regurgitate stomach oil through mouth and nostrils. The function of this discharge, which occurs when the bird is alarmed, or stimulated in some way such as by the appearance of a predator or its mate, and in preening and chick-feeding, is somewhat puzzling. In composition it resembles the preen gland oil, and the spermaceti oil of whales. It is rich in vitamins A and D; and turns to wax when cold. It appears to be a dietary residue of the petrel's oil-rich fish and crustacean food, accumulated after the digestion of the more soluble protein component. The oil is stored in the epithetial cells (walls or mucosa) of the proventriculus or glandular region of stomach, which is large and much folded longitudinally like a collapsed balloon. It has an unpleasantly strong musky odour which clings persistently to the petrel and its nesting place (and to human flesh and clothes when an observer handles any petrel). In the fulmers, including the giant fulmar (appropriately named stinker), the evil-smelling fluid may shoot several feet towards the visitor, as if deliberately aimed; although it is more likely that it travels in that direction because the bird is facing towards him, ready to defend itself with the hooked bill, which is opened threateningly. The main function of this vomiting is to lighten the bird for easier escape. The skunk-like habit of squirting a stinking fluid at intruders may have developed therefore as a supplementary defence in the fulmars, which nest in open vulnerable situations.

The oil appears only in the stomachs of nestling petrels, and disappears therefrom later, when the chicks are bigger and are being fed more solid semi-digested marine organisms; it is in effect a store of baby-food of the right consistency. It has also been suggested that it serves the adult, thirsty during the typically long spells of incubation and brooding alone at the nest, as reserve 'physiological water', camel-fashion. Despite its powerful smell, it is perfectly digestible, and used in preparation of food by Polynesian and other peoples.

SWIMMING AND DIVING

Adaptations for swimming and diving are numerous and varied. At the surface the feet are used almost exclusively for propulsion, normally by alternate strokes, as in walking. For this purpose all truly oceanic birds are assisted by webs between the toes, which are modified according to the method of hunting for food. In gannets, cormorants and pelicans all four toes are joined by broad webs for fast swimming under water. Penguins have thick clumsy-looking feet, three toes joined by two webs, the fourth (hind) toe being rudimentary; but they do not normally use the feet in fast underwater chase except as a rudder. Gulls, skuas and terns, which make only shallow dives, have elegant feet with smaller webs adapted to limited surface swimming, and to walking nimbly on land. In phalaropes the webs are reduced to flanges or lobes each side of the three forward toes—an abbreviation possibly adapted to facilitate its habit of fast twirling of the body in feeding at the surface? Large heavy sea birds (albatrosses, gannets, cormorants) use the webbed feet effectively to lever against the water as they taxi forward in taking flight.

In order to swim under the sea the specific gravity of a bird must be only a little less than that of salt water. Various devices in diving birds enable them to overcome normal buoyancy which keeps them afloat on the surface when at rest, or at will. Air is automatically expelled from the lungs and numerous air sacs within the body. The plumage is compressed by muscular contraction, and, as the bird descends, by the increasing pressure of water; both expel the air trapped in the feathers, further reducing buoyancy. But oxygen is essential to keep the central nervous system functioning, and as the lungs have been emptied oxygen is liberated from the blood (the oxyhaemoglobin and oxymyoglobin in the muscles), helped by accumulating carbon dioxide gas produced by metabolic heat. Under water, too, the body is cooler, and the heart beats about ten times more slowly during suspended breathing, so restricting the flow of blood and loss of energy. Again, the bones of diving birds are less pneumatised, more solid, than those of land birds, and this enables them to float lower at the surface, and sink more easily. On average diving birds remain underwater for less than one minute. Their rib cages are stronger than those of land birds, to withstand pressure.

Penguins show extreme adaptations for diving. At the surface they float nearly submerged, because they have heavy bones, no air sacs, and trap little air between the short dense body feathers. Blood heat is maintained by the thick layer of sub-

North Atlantic gannets migrate as far south as tropical seas off West Africa; the speckling on the wings indicates immaturity

cutaneous fat, which has a lower specific gravity than salt water. Their shortened wings have no quill feathers, and have become modified to serve the same propulsive functions as the front flippers of seals.

Auks and diving petrels, which fly lumberingly and with apparent reluctance, progress under water expertly, if somewhat jerkily, by a restricted form of flapping flight, the wings not fully opened: the primary feathers of the outer wing or 'hand' are closed together to form a strong paddle. Hunting cormorants, on the other hand, move under water with wings tightly folded into the body feathers, and are propelled by the broad webbed feet used with the motion of a sculling oar; they search for fish close to the bottom with long neck extended clear of the turbulence of their own wake, which might stir up detritus and cloud the water behind them.

The diving of tropic birds, gannets and boobies is described later. They sight fish from the air, and rely on the impetus of the head-first plunge to surprise and capture. The dagger-shaped bill and thick skull bones are adapted to ease penetration and resist shock, which is further absorbed by the thick cushion of neck feathers above the (probably inflated) air sacs of the upper breast. Just before impact the wings are flattened and trailed vertically in line with the tail, reducing friction.

31

These birds are too buoyant to dive deep (see page 132). In birds which swim under water both the webbed feet and the (usually short) tail are used in steering. A long tail seems of little advantage under water: the plunge-diving tropic bird with ornamental tail as long as its body is an indifferent swimmer, and leaves the water quickly, while the frigate bird never enters it—its long tail is for aerial gymnastics above the water. The darter, a riverine and swamp cormorant appropriately known as snake bird, perhaps needs its long tail to balance its excessively long neck, and in its snake-like swimming amid submerged vegetation.

THE SENSES

Sight is the most important of the senses. Living normally in a world of bright light over the sea, the eyes of oceanic birds are usually rather small, placed laterally at the sides of the head, giving a wide visual field of about 340°. Gannets have frontally placed, very mobile eyes, giving a smaller visual field but a large binocular concentration for plunge-diving. Crepuscular and night-feeding birds (some gulls,

North Atlantic gannet plunge diving for fish below the surface of the sea

skimmers) have slightly larger eyes; the skimmers are unique among birds in having the pupil appear as a vertical slit, as in cats. Most amphibious birds are short-sighted in air; their eyes are perfectly adapted for seeing under water. The lens is softer and bulges forward to accommodate the maximum amount of light. All birds have a nictitating membrane, a semi-transparent third lid which is drawn horizontally across the eye from the nasal side; laden with tears, this cleans and lubricates the cornea, and may be used to protect the eye in bad weather and under the water, although it reduces the light reaching the lens. To overcome this several diving birds (auks, divers, ducks) have a clean lens-like window in the centre of the membrane, which acts in effect like a contact lens. Nothing is new under the sun— here we see windscreen wiper complete with water-brush, and contact lens, in the small eye of a bird!

Birds have a higher range of *hearing* (40 to 29,000 cycles per second) than man (16 to 20,000 cps); otherwise their sense of hearing, construction of ear, with its balancer mechanism, do not differ greatly from those of mammals. Like man, they recognise individuals of their own species by voice. At sea the excited cries of others at a shoal of fish draw sea birds to join the feast, but it is likely that the gathering was first noticed by sight. Hearing is not so important in oceanic birds. Some birds call to each other on migration (terns, waders), others are silent at sea most of the time (petrels, auks).

The usually small olfactory lobes in the average bird's brain suggest a poor sense of *smell*, which seems to be the case in oceanic birds, which do not need to follow scent trails or hunt for food on land. The nasal passages and chambers, are well developed however. The two frontal chambers clean and moisten the air inhaled in breathing; in sea birds excess salt is discharged in solution into the first chamber, as described above. Some birds have a strong odour (petrels, puffins) but there is no evidence that this assists individual recognition in those species. The large nostrils of the petrel family have several functions, as already mentioned (see also page 29), and the third chamber, containing the olfactory receptors connecting with the brain, is well developed, as also the lobe itself. Murphy (1936) considers that albatrosses and other petrels, and skuas, can detect edible fat, offal, meat, and blood floating on the surface of the sea by their sense of smell. Albatross, cape pigeon and giant fulmar appeared rapidly when strong-smelling heated oil or fat was trailed behind a ship.

The sense of *taste* is poorly developed in birds, which have no teeth to masticate and 'enjoy' food in the mouth. Man has about 9,000 taste buds distributed over his tongue and mouth parts; birds have less than 100, confined to the soft parts under the horny tongue. Solid food is gulped down with little tasting; but in drinking, fluids reach the taste buds, and in experimental tests thirsty birds showed preferences for some chemical solutions and rejected others. During the moment that a bird captures fish or takes other food into the mouth, it is best able to *test* it through the scent molecules in fluid exudations from the prey reaching the taste buds below the tongue, and by the odour of the food which, so long as it is held in the mouth, is inhaled with the air reaching the olfactory receptors in the third chamber, conveniently open nearest the roof of the mouth. Gustatory satisfaction in birds derives largely during swallowing of food and its early digestion in the *crop*, which is richly furnished with mucous and salivary glands—just that satisfaction of feeling comfortably full we experience after a good meal.

33

(*Facing page*) Red-billed tropic bird, Tower Island, Galapagos

Protective or *cryptic* coloration is less common as a selective adaptation and advantage in oceanic than in land birds. Several polar species breeding against a background of snow and ice are nearly or completely white (snow petrel, sheathbill, ivory gull, and there is a white phase in the giant fulmar breeding on or near the antarctic continent). The dull dark-coloured upper plumage of many of the smaller hole-nesting shearwaters and petrels renders them less conspicuous to aerial predators at sea, and more particularly when they come ashore at night.

Conspicuous or *phaneric* coloration: the white plumage of gannets, boobies, some terns, gulls and other social species, is conspicuous against the sky, and serves as a signal in fishing and other aerial movements. Many amphibious birds have white underparts, which may be an adaptation for feeding under water, by rendering them less conspicuous to fish prey below them; on the other hand it has been suggested that, like the gleam from silver-coloured metal bait of a fishing line trailed through the water, the flash of reflected light from white plumage may deceive fish and draw them towards the predator. Sunlight can also be reflected under the surface from iridescent dark plumage: the cormorant hunting along the sea bed is said to attract fish by the flash of light reflected from the glossy black nape of its snaking neck.

Kittiwakes, common guillemots and razorbills sharing steep cliffs; note the guillemot variant with white spectacles

The value of bright colours in courtship and reproductive activities is discussed in the next chapter, and under species.

The interesting genetic mechanism of morphism occurs in sea birds where, in a single interbreeding population, two (*dimorphism*) or more (*polymorphism*) distinguishable morphological forms or behaviour patterns regularly co-exist. For example, plumage colour, which is determined by the hereditary genes in the feather germ, varies from dark to light phases in the skuas and in certain shearwaters and petrels. Attempts to correlate these interbreeding phases with temperature and latitude (white to the north, as in polar *species*, quoted above; black to the south, as in *races* of man) are quite unsatisfactory, although there is apparent local stability (a kind of quivering balance) in the colour ratio. Thus, as discussed in Chapter 9, fulmars are generally (almost 100 per cent in some localities) blue-breasted in their arctic breeding grounds, and white-breasted in the southern limit of nesting, with intermediates between. Conversely, about three-quarters of arctic skuas or jaegers are pale in the north, and dusky in the south. In the pomarine skua the ratio does not vary with latitude: at all its widespread breeding grounds the light form of this jaeger predominates by about 6 to 1.

The white eye-spectacle or bridle of the Atlantic guillemot or murre is a morph which increases in frequency with latitude, and apparently with humidity, from nil in southern Europe to above fifty per cent in the Barents Sea of the Arctic Ocean. Yet its Pacific subspecies has no bridled phase! The relative advantages of these colour phases, more or less randomly distributed between the sexes of a single breeding group, are far from clear.

Sexual dimorphism—differences between male and female appearance or behaviour—is easier to understand. In most species of oceanic birds adult males and females are so alike externally that it is impossible for the observer to distinguish them visually except by recognisable male or female behaviour. Even voices may seem identical. The male is often, but not always, larger than the female; he is smaller in the bluefoot booby. Monogamy is the rule in these species, where the sexes are alike in appearance. Polygamy (inherited dimorphic sexual behaviour) is associated with brilliant-coloured males and drab females; but the male frigate or man of war bird is an exception. Despite the huge scarlet pouch which distinguishes him from the pouchless female, he is faithful to his mate and a good father to the single chick in the nest. He is sexually dimorphic by his different colour, and in deserting the chick at fledging time—the female continues to feed it for several more weeks.

Polyandry, another form of dimorphic sexual behaviour, is very rare in birds, but it occurs in the phalarope. The female is more brightly coloured than the male, mates with more than one male, and does not incubate, or care for the young.

BILL ADAPTATIONS

Bird bills have more functions than the human mouth has. Primarily the bill is a tool or hand to pick up food, and secondarily to build a nest, preen, and as a defensive weapon. It is often highly coloured—an adaptation to display.

In many sea birds it is long and pointed for swift seizure and swallowing above or under water (gannets, some auks, terns). In the darters the bill is a sword for impaling a fish, which must be removed, sometimes with difficulty, before it can be swallowed.

(*Facing page*) Great frigate bird; male displaying with its inflated throat pouch

C

Cormorant

Wandering Albatross

Puffin

Razorbill

Guillemot

Great Frigate Bird

Gannet

Yellow-billed Tropic Bird

Great Skua

Sandwich Tern

Grey Phalarope

NOT DRAWN TO SCALE

(*Facing page*) Bill adaptations

In shags and cormorants the bill is long, the upper mandible being strongly hooked at the tip, serving as a forceps for gripping and lifting upwards. In pelicans, gannets and boobies, the upper mandible tip is curved only just sufficiently to screen the tip of the lower, so protecting the mouth from being forced open on striking the water in the violent dive. Gannets and boobies swallow fish at once, but pelicans will collect several fish as they work in concert rounding up a shoal, scooping with their broad bill and storing them in the landing net of the enormous pouch attached to the lower mandible. Water is expelled from the pouch by pressing it against the curved neck, the bill almost closed, before the head is thrown upwards and the catch gulped down.

In the petrels, which are principally surface feeders, making only shallow dives, both mandibles of the medium long bill curve downwards at the tip, which has a slight gap when closed; the very sharp tip of the upper mandible, which is strengthened by a thick horny shield above, pierces the food while the lower tip crushes; the grip is enormously strong, inflicting a lacerating wound upon the human hand unfortunate enough to be grasped by a shearwater or large petrel during banding or other operations in a colony. In some (whale birds, cape pigeon) which feed on plankton, the bill is broadened at the throat, with a pouch to hold a large quantity of food, as in the pelicans; but the water is strained and the minute organisms retained by a comb-like ridge of lamellae or teeth along the cutting edges of the bill, the large fleshy tongue assisting the process.

Gulls and skuas have developed a chisel-shaped bill for stabbing and hammering. Individual gulls, failing to open a tough bivalve (cockle, mussel, clam), will carry it aloft and drop it on a hard surface, so that it cracks, but occasionally miss out and drop it on sand; this is an acquired (learned) habit.

The auks show a wide range of bill adaptations unusual in a single family. The common guillemot or murre has a gannet-like beak for grasping a single fish longer than its bill. The razorbill has a more wedge-shaped beak for grasping and holding several small fishes at the same time. This is carried to the extreme in the puffin, with its highly decorative coloured bill, which is cone-shaped in profile and flattened vertically; and during under-water pursuit it is able to catch and hold between ten and thirty small fishes in one load for its chick. The roof of the mouth and the tongue are grooved with small projections (retroverted papillae) pointing inwards which assist retention of the first-caught fish during the underwater chase. The rich colouring and the horny or fleshy appendages of the puffin's bill and face, however, are functional only in courtship display. The decorative basal sheath of the bill, the fleshy mouth rosette, and horny eye-patches, are shed after the breeding season, and in winter the puffin is comparatively drab in appearance.

Another somewhat grotesque-looking adaptation is the shortening of the rigid upper mandible of the long bill of the skimmer or scissorsbill; the flexible lower mandible projects one third more. With long wings held high above the body, the skimmer flies low over the calm evening or night sea, bill open and lower mandible ploughing the surface, shovelling marine organisms into its mouth, often creating a sparkling luminescent wake.

3 BEHAVIOUR

In simplest terms, initial behaviour in the new-born animal is controlled by instinctive 'knowledge' of what to do in a presented situation in order to survive: not a process of reasoning or thinking as we know it, but a purely innate physiological reaction to stimuli—the reflex action of earlier students of animal behaviour, and in man demonstrated by the baby's reaction of sucking when presented with the soft warm flesh of the human body. The infant senses feed each impression automatically to the computer of the brain and nervous system, already programmed to respond to these electrical signals of impulses in a specific way by the genetical codes which the primordial cell has acquired from its parents at the fusion of sperm with ovum.

In many of the lower invertebrates there is little or no development of intelligence or learning after birth as an independent organism. It is enough to survive— further development is inessential, if not dangerous to the existing pattern of nature (as in horror films when an insect becomes an intelligent man-devouring giant); the brainless virus which develops greater virulence is bad enough from man's point of view. But in mammals, birds, reptiles, and fish, further chemical and electronic development and changes occur in the memory cells during life, known as learning; combined with the innate processes, these enable the higher vertebrates to regulate their lives with a degree of reasoning more or less akin to that in man.

Adult sea-bird behaviour is controlled by this mixture of much instinct and little learning, evolved through natural selection of the fittest individual to survive and breed. The physiological or 'proximate' factors for success include good health and an accurate timing mechanism which ensure the bird is fit and ready to breed at the most favourable time of year for the raising of young. 'Ultimate' factors are the right environment of food and safe breeding site.

SOCIAL BEHAVIOUR

The bird receives its first lesson in social behaviour before it leaves the egg. It is believed that towards the end of the incubation period the chick's movements inside the unbroken shell are recognised by the brooding parent: the actions of the adult usually include solicitous touching movements with bill and breast, and low vocal response to the chick's first muffled cheeping. This 'imprinting' of the adult voice on the receptive memory cells of the infant brain is the primary, indelible lesson in learning. Sensitivity to voice (hearing) is more important than sight at first. This is demonstrated in some burrow-nesting species: the chick, born in the darkness of a deep tunnel, may never see its parents clearly before they abandon it when it is full-grown (some hole-nesting auks, petrels, shearwaters). But it 'learns the language' of its species before they do so.

Shortly after hatching the young sea bird of most species also learns to recognise the individual voice of each parent; and if it is born in a noisy colony of many pairs of its kind it will respond only to their calls. Conversely the parents are able to recognise, and be guided by, the individual voice of their chick or chicks. It is unlikely that the chick recognises the sex of a parent—that is a matter of trial and error at a more mature age. But in some species the chick early recognises its parents as individuals from their distinctive behaviour (for example, the male gull feeding the female who in turn feeds the chick) and voices, differences also detectable by the human observer.

Each action of brooding, feeding, preening and voice by the adults serves to

The handsome Sabine's gull at nest

strengthen the social (family) bond, and the chick learns to associate these imprinted pleasures of being warmed, fed and cared for with close contact with others of its kind. Its developing behaviour is thus a mixture of innate responses and of learning, or maturation of learning, in the early hours or days of its life. In diurnally active species sight recognition quickly follows.

However, voice recognition remains important for survival in the unpleasant situation of danger to life which can arise at any time during the chick's dependence on the adults, and in later life. On the approach of a predator or other disturbance the adult utters a special loud warning cry, and adopts an alert attitude, or flies away. The chick's response is innate and automatic; and a single vocal warning by one adult can alert and draw the appropriate response from all neighbours within hearing. The chick's reaction to danger can begin within a few hours of birth in nidifugous birds, ie those born with eyes open and a covering of down, and able to leave the nest with their parents soon after, such as waders, game birds, and some gulls and terns; the response in these youngsters is to 'freeze' where they are, in or out of the nest, a wonderful adaptation to survival by concealment: their cryptic colouring blends them with their environment as long as they do not move. They stay still until the parent sounds the all-clear, a different, quieter call.

But in nidicolous species, whose young are hatched with eyes closed and are apparently helpless (some naked), such as cormorants, gannets, pelicans and some of the petrels (these are born with down), there is no response to danger for several days; and until its eyes are wide open and a thick coat of down has covered the

Arctic skua at nest in northern Europe

nestling, it seems unable to recognise danger. Even then it remains in the nest, and its only defence, in the absence of its parents, which have escaped by flight, is to stab towards an intruder, uttering threatening noises.

The young bird learns to recognise the meaning of the various sounds uttered by its parents, which convey information about food, enemies, and domestic affairs. Although it may not be able to produce these sounds recognisably until its own sound-box (syrinx) has matured, it undoubtedly remembers them faithfully for future use. (Male song birds born and reared in complete isolation do not develop the full song of the free wild males, but do so on hearing it later.)

In some gregarious sea birds, where there is a heavy concentration of nests on level or sloping ground, the growing chicks leave the nest at a certain age (2-3 days in royal and sandwich terns, 4 weeks in some penguins) and gather into a group, known as a crèche. During calm peaceful conditions the crèche is loosely spread out and relaxed, with a number of apparently idle adults in attendance. But on the appearance of a predator (including man) the chicks coalesce, and the crèche may move away from the source of disturbance in a tight bunch, the adults forming a bodyguard (penguins) or flying and dive-bombing above the intruder (terns). Crèche-forming has a further survival function during bad weather: the chicks huddle warmly together and so better withstand cold, storm, drifting snow or sand.

Sea birds nesting colonially on cliffs and broken ground (gannets, albatrosses, some gulls and auks) do not form crèches. It would be too dangerous for the young flightless birds to herd together in precipitous situations, and instead the adults fiercely repel any attempt by avian visitors to enter the few square feet or less of nesting territory. One or two oceanic birds adopt a remarkable method of nest defence known as distraction display: the male phalarope, and the jaegers (small skuas) simulate injury and stagger and tumble along the ground until the would-be predator has been drawn far away from the eggs or chicks (page 140).

ADOLESCENCE

The moment of fledging is the time of greatest mortality in the young birds, inexperienced in obtaining food and avoiding attack by predators. The young petrel, shearwater or puffin, deserted and solitary in its dark hole in the ground, must find its way to the sea alone. This it does instinctively by night, so avoiding diurnal predators; and, guided by the same purely innate knowledge of what to do next, will swim and fly quite rapidly, alone, to reach the wintering ground of the adults. Perhaps fifty per cent will fall by the way from various causes—starvation, storm, predation. On catching up with the wide-ranging adult flock in winter quarters, it is unlikely that the juvenile petrel or puffin will meet its parents, but if it does they will hardly recognise it. Its voice and plumage will have matured in the interval, and in any case they will not have seen each other clearly before in the bright light of day. Further during its first lone swimming and flying experience (tropic birds, gannets, puffins and most petrels) it will have learned that adult birds of all kinds, even its own species, are indifferent and generally hostile to its approaches, whether deliberate or accidental, and may attempt to kill it. It is impossible to generalise however, because while some young birds appear to have an inbuilt aggressiveness to repel attack, others are timid and escape from danger by flying or diving.

In contrast the young of several species of gull, tern, guillemot, booby and frigate bird remain dependent for food on one or both adults for many days and weeks, perhaps months, after leaving their birthplace. These immatures may follow, or be convoyed by, parents in shared fishing expeditions (some auks) and local migration; or may hang about near the roosting place, waiting and calling plaintively for food (boobies, gulls, frigate birds), but rebuffed if they approach birds other than their parents.

At weaning time the intense social behaviour and family ties at the nest are thus modified by the awareness of danger. The young bird learns to maintain what has been called safety or individual distance between itself and the nearest individuals. The threat signals of the adults not only taught it to retreat before the aggressive advance of more powerful birds, but to employ the same intimidating postures and calls to drive away birds weaker than itself. Aggressive display, part instinctive, part copied from the adults, varies considerably, but most species adopt a typical crouching position, wings partly spread, head lowered, neck hackles rising, the bill directed at the opponent and open to utter threat cries. In some species the mouth has a vividly coloured palate, which increases the effect.

In bird flocks, even at sea, there is a definite order of precedence, with the strongest, most aggressive, individual at the top of the hierarchy or peck order. In fulmar petrels watched feeding at the side of a trawler off Rockall, 150 miles west of the Outer Hebrides, I noticed how one or two individuals drove others away and secured for themselves the site below the scuppers where the fish offal trickled into the sea. There was also interspecific competition: great shearwaters displaying aggressively at fulmars over the same titbits of offal.

In the peck order of the winter flock at sea the juvenile has a low initial status, as in communities of man. But it will move up as it matures and becomes more experienced. In the spring, when the established breeders depart early for the nesting grounds, and the majority of immature birds remain behind in the wintering zone, new young leaders doubtless emerge; but little is known about the psychological relationships between individuals in the pelagic flocks.

STIMULUS TO BREEDING

Given an adequate food supply, once the moult is completed the bird is in a favourable condition to breed. It is likely that photo-periodism—the regulation of the physiological cycle by the amount of daylight available—is a principal external stimulus to breeding, especially in temperate and high latitudes, where day-length increases more rapidly in the spring than at the equator. This seems a good rule, but has its exceptions. The emperor and king penguins in the Antarctic, and some shearwaters in cool temperate latitudes, begin to breed in the chill weather of autumn, and incubate and raise young over the winter. In the tropics, where day and night are nearly equal in length, a number of terns, boobies, petrels and other birds have no exact breeding season, but nest whenever food and territory are optimally available.

However, the majority of sea birds in the higher latitudes do breed in the long daylight of spring and summer, which incidentally gives them a longer day in which to collect food if they are diurnal and rest by night. An adequately rich food supply is necessary to nourish and activate the endocrine system (glands of internal secretion) which feed hormones and other chemical components into the blood stream and

Prolonged nesting operations of the wandering albatross extending over more than one year result in only one chick being reared in two years

initiate gonad development, resulting in ovulation in the female and spermatogenesis in the male. The most important gland for the production of sex hormones is the anterior pituitary, at the base of the skull, which appears to be linked with the intrinsic periodicity or seasonal rhythm of the bird's behaviour pattern. The bird is governed by rhythm, by the ticking of its biological clock, which began with its first heart-beats (the 'second' hand, up to 5 ticks per second in sea birds) in the egg; by the repetitious activity of each twenty-four hours, involving regular feeding and rest periods (circadian rhythm), and by the cycle of seasonal behaviour described in this chapter. So exact is this sense of time that many sea birds breeding in high latitudes (eg muttonbirds studies on the Bass Strait islands) lay their egg on or about the same day each year.

The right food (including food for the young) at the right season, and in the right environment is the primary stimulus to reproduction. But the impulse to mate arising therefrom reaches its intensity for only a brief period in the breeding cycle, and it is vitally important that it be synchronised in the individual and species to take the maximum advantage of these benign local conditions while they last. This is achieved by the secondary stimulus of courtship display.

DISPLAY IN SEA BIRDS

When the young bird, stimulated by the development of its gonads, returns to the nesting ground to breed for the first time, it has to 'undo learning' and overcome a formidable barrier—the habit of individual or safety distance, already described—in order to copulate with a partner. The inexperienced individual may fail to overcome it in the season of its first return. In that case its behaviour remains appetitive: it arrives, establishes a territory (however inadequate), displays and flirts with a bird of the opposite sex. It may not even touch another bird, but if it does copulate, it does so too late to rear a family. This behaviour is however functional: it has familiarised itself with a suitable breeding site, and met a prospective future partner.

In mature sea birds the male arrives and occupies the site first. He may begin building a nest. He calls loudly at intervals. In the untried breeder the actions are automatic and imitative: he has no clear idea why he is behaving in this way, and may not recognise the sex of his first visitor. The old experienced male is more knowledgeable; he has recognised the site and awaits a female to join him. If she is his mate of yesteryear he remembers (recognises) her promptly; in that case the preliminary ceremonies of breaking down safety distance are brief, and touching contact soon established. So it is an advantage to mate for life, since this means earlier breeding, and greater rearing success, as Coulson found in kittiwake gulls.

The origins of courtship display, involving the use of the bill in appetitive fencing, rubbing, gaping and preening motions, can be traced to similar movements used in feeding and being fed and preened as a chick. Love and hate, or fear, drives are apparent in the sexual display. Threatening attitudes appear, also derived from the chick's part-instinctive, part-learned behaviour of defending itself from rivals (as when contending with its nest mates for food), and marauders (alien adults of the same or other species). On arrival at the nest site one partner may be attacked at first by the other in an automatic temporary reassertion of the fear or defensive reaction; recognition quickly follows, confirmed by voice, and by typical submissive actions of the female turning aside the head to hide the aggressive bill.

In the monogamous sea birds, male and female are so alike externally in plumage and colour that it is hardly surprising that sex and mate recognition are preceded by threat display, in case the visitor is a stranger. Usually the incoming bird calls loudly, signalling its identity before arrival; even so, the welcome by its partner will have elements of threat in it: the reaction has become a habit. There is a vast literature describing the varied and fascinating courtship displays of birds, carried to fantastic intensity in male birds-of-paradise with their spectacular, superbly coloured plumage, and associated with polygamy in these and other species in which the male is more brightly coloured than the female. The more sober displays of oceanic birds, which are monogamous, are discussed in detail in the life-history chapters later in this book.

The so-called love ceremonies, which take place when mated birds are at the nest together, are mutual and continue throughout the breeding season, even with young in the nest. They serve as the physical stimulus to synchronize mating, and afterwards as a strong emotional bond to keep the pair interested in each other, and so in the common, perhaps monotonous, task of feeding and protecting the young. They usually consist of nibbling and preening actions, accompanied by bursts of vocal activity, which also serves to warn neighbours that the nest is occupied and will be defended.

Mutual preening in mated birds is less a function of cleaning than a sublimated activity. As gannets nibble each other's necks and heads, they do not, except accidentally, apply the waxy oil from the preen gland to their mate's feathers. The action is a substitute for the unaltruistic drives of aggression (dominance), possessiveness (of territory), and above all, sexual desire. Early in the breeding season the male gannet will preen the golden head feathers of his mate until he obtains a grip on the nape, when he may then attempt to mount and copulate. The mutual 'necking' of male and female in human courtship, serving no function of hygiene, clearly has the same excitatory function as in gannets, maintaining the emotional bond.

DISPLACEMENT ACTIVITY

Display, mutual or otherwise, is thus closely linked with so-called displacement actions, which are a substitute for the normal performance of a quite different intention. They arise from frustration of this intention; as, for example, when an incoming bird wishing to brood picks up a stone or twig, holds it in the bill (gulls, puffins), throws it into the air and catches it again, as if playfully (gannets, cormorants), or places it on the nest rim, while its mate obstinately continues to occupy the coveted nest. On its own a brooding bird, perhaps bored or complacently happy, or wishing to leave the nest but unwilling to do so until relieved by its mate, will release tension by leaning forward and pulling nest material over its back or close around it (a function of nest building). Probably from this displacement activity has evolved a nest-covering ritual with survival value, notably in ducks and grebes; and the male phalarope will bend grasses to form a bower over the nest. In brooding the bird is performing a natural useful function; any other activity at the same time is distractive, but not meaningless; at least it uses up surplus energy, and might have an adaptive value. Useless, non-adaptive behaviour tends to die out in nature.

Another example of simultaneous arousal of incomplete drive and substitute

behaviour patterns is that of rival gulls defending nesting territory. Like gamecocks about to fight, they will pluck grass and earth furiously as in nest-building or feeding behaviour, while the level of testerone rises rapidly in the blood, as in man facing danger. In the meantime they are, in fact, attacking the ground instead— this is redirected attack. Bulls paw the ground, dogs scratch earth and grass backwards, men will kick chairs, all in redirected attack, a true displacement activity. In puffins, which can fight each other viciously with bill and claw, frequent fighting in this social and sociable species would be disadvantageous, and a substitute is found in the action of mutual pushing and rubbing of the huge bills together, with all the appearance of friendliness and enjoyment, which occurs between both mated pairs and unrelated individuals as they rest or stroll around idly in their afternoon assemblies on the island cliffs. Single birds will 'let off steam' by carrying a stone or straw around, or furiously digging a hole (redirected attack?), or plucking a mouthful of maritime flowers (a comical sight!); the impulse presently waning, it will drop the object, which perhaps another will pick up. More than most sea birds, puffins seem to enjoy life.

It is easier to describe display and apparent displacement activity than to explain it adequately; it is still a subject of great interest and continuing research.

FLOCKING

Flocking in sea birds is believed to be a social 'tendency' rather than a purely innate activity, partly because in animals of gregarious habit, from bees and fish to birds and bison, it can be learned by example from infancy. Most of those sea birds which form dense communities at the breeding site tend to maintain a loose association at sea, spread out but generally within sight of each other when feeding or on migration. The solitary nesters (some albatrosses, gulls, tropic birds) are more often encountered singly at sea. Adélie penguins bunch together at sea, diving, 'porpoising', bathing, and fishing in regimental style.

Flocking is a stimulating activity and has considerable survival value. At sea, flocks of more than one species mingle in the search for food, and will come together upon a shoal of fish or other visible marine food, as vultures will converge upon carrion from a wide radius of hunting territory. The competition where the same food species is taken is more apparent than real. As described in Chapter 2, each species fishes by a different method, usually capturing different sizes of fish or different organisms associated with the shoal. At the breeding site there is better protection where many nests are close together. Predators arriving from the air face difficulty in raiding effectively amongst tightly grouped adults on nest guard. The larger the colony the smaller the proportion of vulnerable boundary nests to total breeding pairs. Many observations have shown that the larger colonies normally have the greatest breeding success. The presence of so many sexually mature birds close together, displaying and calling, is highly stimulating, and promotes the synchronisation of copulation (sometimes to the extent that a wave of coition will ripple through a colony), and so of egg-laying, within a short period so that eggs and young are at risk for less time. Although large noisy colonies attract local predators, there are more adults available to harry and even strike them; defence methods vary, as already indicated. In gulls, terns and skuas several adults will swoop at the intruder, one after another, but it is noticeable that each attacking bird in reality is defending only the territory of its nesting site, and desists when the visitor moves elsewhere within the colony, when other birds take up the attack in turn. Those social species which lack agility in flight (albatross, gannet, auks) do not attempt aerial mobbing of enemies, the adult instead defending its own nest by threat display—typically opening of wings, lunging with bill, and alarm cries. This is often more effective than aerial mobbing, since the eggs or chicks are not

North Atlantic gannet; the chick is heavier than the adult and will be deserted at fledging time

The wonderer of the ocean

49

exposed. (I have sometimes thought, when trying to avoid the dagger beak during banding operations in a large gannetry, that if only the mass of adults had combined to attack me I could not have survived!)

Where predation is severe, or other factors are causing a declining population in a breeding flock, the exact density per square yard or metre is nevertheless normally maintained year by year, so long as the group survives. In spite of the availability of suitable territory near by, the social sea birds prefer to crowd together in a specific and fixed pattern. Thus gannets, increasing from 60 to over 30,000 adults in a hundred years on the islet of Grassholm, Wales, have continued to compete for sites within the original colony and to expand outwards around its perimeter at the same ratio of density, approximately one nest to one square metre. As a result 15,000 pairs occupy only about 3 acres of this 22 acre islet, the whole surface of which appears suitable terrain for nesting. Conversely, guillemots which from time immemorial occupied a wide ledge some 200 yards long on the cliffs of neighbouring Skomer Island, have decreased of late years, and instead of spreading out thinly over the ledge have moved together to form two or three typically concentrated breeding flocks, each pair about a foot apart. The gaps between are not even visited, and have become overgrown with chickweed, tolerant of the ancient guano deposit.

In general the ground plan of group-nesting in sea birds is determined by the minimum territorial requirements of the breeding pair. An individual dying or disappearing from the centre is immediately replaced from the outer ranks. The breeding flock is normally composed of a core of old adults; fully mature, they have arrived first in the season and claimed the long established, least vulnerable, centre nest sites. They are flanked by a bulk of middle-aged members, and an outer ring of less experienced young adults, last to return to breed, must perforce take up the exposed positions. If they survive in the years ahead, these birds will return earlier each year, and move towards the centre as the old adults die. However, if only one of a central pair returns, an unattached bird will make up the loss. In successful colonies of gannets, skuas, gulls and penguins, the gap early in the season is immediately filled by pairs from a 'club' or reservoir of unemployed birds outside the colony.

Where a social species has expanded in numbers so that no apparently suitable nesting territory is available within the occupied terrain, the young adults seeking to breed for the first time must look elsewhere. It seems clear, from banding results and field observation, that it is the young adults which seek and colonise new sites. (However, it is not always lack of suitable nesting space near the mother colony that induces this colonisation; over-fishing of local waters causing food shortage is another factor.) But in settling at a new site the young colonists may be several seasons before successfully raising young for the first time. Cut off from the protection and stimulus of the large flock and exposed to predation, they often fail, and disappear from the site. In social nesting species, two or three pairs together normally produce more young per adult than one pair breeding alone.

Stimulation and protection, resulting in better success in a low number of colonising individuals, can however be given by the presence of other gregarious species; for example, a small number of gulls or terns of one species may nest within a large colony of another species of tern or gull, and a few pairs of the intensely social common guillemot or murre have been found nesting successfully

Kittiwakes on narrow cliff ledges defend their nests vocally, but seldom fight

in the middle of a large gannetry (Alderney, Channel Islands; and Grassholm). Conversely two pairs of gannets bred successfully for many years in the centre of a large colony of auks on Great Saltee Island.

DEFENCE OF TERRITORY

The main function of territorial behaviour in birds is of course to secure isolation in which to survive and breed. In some flocks, notably some terns, and penguins, territory appears to belong to the whole colony rather than the individual or pair. The individual is vocal but not pugnacious. Royal, sandwich, common and arctic terns show minimal neighbour aggression and territory defence when breeding, although nests are often so close that one sitting bird can touch the next. This sociable behaviour may be linked with the habit of forming crèches when the young are a few days old; and with the tendency to abandon a communal nesting site suddenly and completely, even in the middle of egg-laying, if the colony is much disturbed by predators or visiting humans. Attachment to the site is loose until incubation is well advanced. On the appearance of man, all the adult terns will rise simultaneously, and there is a dramatic silence for a moment as they move in a cloud through the sky. Then the screaming calls break out, as if the parliament were deciding what the next move should be. Normally the sociable terns, conspicuous and noisy, nest on small islands or headlands free of mammalian predators; but if a disturbance through predation, high tide, or exceptional gales seriously reduces breeding success, the colony will survive as a unit by selecting another (presumably more favourable) site for the next egg-laying cycle, perhaps a replacement laying in the same season—but in the latter case the delay in time may be fatal to breeding success.

4 OCEAN FEEDING
GROUNDS

As the numbers of marine birds are controlled by their food supply, their greatest concentrations must be in those areas where this is most abundant. Even if there is no suitable nesting site near, the truly oceanic wanderers overcome the problem by living far at sea with their food supply during most of their lives. If necessary the breeding adult will fast for several days when impelled to remain at the nest, far from its normal feeding zone, during an incubation or brooding spell; and at the commencement of the breeding season mature birds will spend several days occupying territory, defending it, pairing with their mate, without feeding; the sexual drive has temporarily supplanted other appetites. When one of a mated pair returns from sea to relieve the other at nest, egg or chick guard, in most species it does not feed the fasting bird, which must fly off in search of sustenance alone, and perhaps over many miles of barren waters. Gulls and terns are an exception; the male will feed his mate, but in these birds domestic duties are usually undertaken in short shifts of a few hours only.

The ocean is rich in mineral and organic matter, but the density of organisms on which the larger animals feed varies considerably and is dependent on the regional meteorological conditions, especially on the amount of sunlight, the strength of the wind and the flow of ocean currents. Odd as it may seem, in view of the large numbers of land birds found in the tropics, the hot equatorial regions of the world's deep oceans support fewer sea birds than the temperate and cold latitudes. This is because of an interesting sequence in the ecological chain.

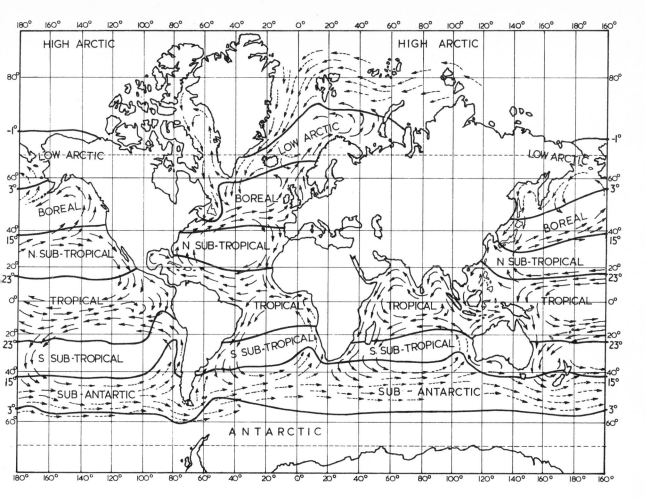

Figure 1 Ocean currents and mean surface temperatures (Celsius) with zones of marine environment

Consider first the west to east rotation of the earth which produces the prevailing trade winds (Figure 1). Theoretically, as the velocity of the earth's surface is greatest (about 1,000 mph) at the equator the movement of the masses of air close to the surface of the sea should be strongest there: the lag or failure of air and water to keep up with the earth's eastward rotation should cause an east to west movement of wind and current—as of course it does, in the form of the predictable trade winds, so important an influence on the migrations of birds.

TRADE WINDS

These are persistent winds which blow from the east between the Tropics of Cancer and Capricorn, dragging the surface waters with them at a slower speed, in a westerly direction. The land masses of the westward continents finally obstruct this free movement of the water, which rises and falls twice each day under the gravitational pull of the sun and moon. Warmed by its passage through the tropics, the trade-wind-driven current is deflected south-west against the land in the southern hemisphere, and north-west in the northern hemisphere. In the Pacific the trade-wind currents thus warm the temperate east coasts of Asia and Australasia; and in the Atlantic the east coasts of the Americas. A similar movement occurs in the Indian Ocean, but more restricted because of the landlocked northern limit.

Moving at first respectively south-west and north-west, then south and north (Figure 1), the warmed waters in both the Pacific and Atlantic (known as the south and north equatorial currents) are next deflected to the east, in the latitudes of the forties. Here they converge with the cold water flowing from polar seas. The strong westerly winds of these latitudes blow as a counter to the equatorial trade winds, producing the movement known as the west-wind-drift in both north and south Pacific and Atlantic, and in the southern Indian, oceans. There is great turbulence where the polar water sinks below the wind-driven warmer water.

Between approximately latitude $45°$S and the antarctic continent at $60°$S, the waters of the three southern oceans mingle unobstructed by land. Here the counter-current of the west-wind-drift is driven unimpeded before an almost incessant westerly gale. The huge mass of water chilled by the icy antarctic climate sweeps east, and north-east, sending fast-moving offshoots of cold water north along the west-facing coasts of South America (the Humboldt Current) and of South Africa (the Benguela Current) which obstruct and divert part of it. Flowing towards the equator these cold currents mingle with the equatorial currents already described. Thus in the southern hemisphere the mass of air and surface water circles in an anticlockwise direction. In the northern hemisphere the complementary movement of surface water is clockwise, but is complicated by the obstructing land masses to the north: the cold counter-currents are not so pronounced or the winds quite so incessant. The movement is warped by the narrow water access to the Arctic Ocean. In the North Pacific cold water trickles south through the narrow Bering Strait to flow as a counter-current to the west-wind-drift south-west along the coast of Kamchatka and northern Japan; and also passes south-east through the Aleutian Islands chain, to cool the western shores of North America, extending its influence to California. In the Atlantic the warm west-wind-drift as it flows east is less restricted by the land mass; instead it is diverted in a northerly direction towards the Arctic by the gap—some 800 miles wide—between Iceland and Scotland. Its influence extends far beyond the Arctic Circle (Figure 4, page 65), providing open water for sea birds all the year as far as $70°$N. In summer boats freely reach Spitzbergen at $80°$N, famous for its multitudes of marine birds, and inhabited by several land mammals, by flowering plants and mosses. By contrast, in the same latitude south, the Antarctic is a frozen lifeless wilderness.

Because of this corridor of warm North Atlantic current penetrating the Arctic Ocean with mild south-westerly winds, conifer forests are able to grow almost to $70°$N in Norway. But the counter-current of arctic water flowing south along the Greenland east coast results in a treeless shore, largely ice-locked, and unvisited except by a few hardy Eskimo hunters. A weak branch of the west-wind-drift (Gulf Stream is an earlier name), however, touches the southern tip of Greenland at Cape Farewell (where low tree growth is possible), and passes north up the west coast beyond the Arctic Circle towards Baffin Bay. On the west side of this narrow waterway a strong current of cold water drains through the huge frozen archipelago of the Canadian Arctic and brings ice and icebergs far south. This is known as the Labrador Current and its convergence with the warm Gulf Stream off Newfound-land produces a turbulent sea famous for its storms, fogs and inexhaustible com-mercial fisheries, especially of cod. Thousands of seals also breed on the drifting sea-ice off this eastern coast of Canada; arctic sea birds winter there, and in summer great numbers of gannets, gulls and auks nest on the sea cliffs.

The sun's light and heat are the basis of all energy on earth and sea; and combining with the chemical components of water, are essential to the growth of such microscopic plant life as algae and diatoms, known as phytoplankton, which are the base of the marine food-chain. Yet although sunlight, so constant at the equator, is essential to the process of photosynthesis, without sufficient mineral nutrients the minute floating plants cannot thrive, nor can the crustaceans which feed on them, nor the fishes, birds, turtles and whales which are the larger links in the chain. These nutrients come from the phosphate, potash and nitrogen of decomposed vegetable and animal life, which in the ocean are produced through the death of organisms ranging from plankton and seaweeds to fish and other animals; from their excrement; and from mineral elements dissolved from rocks and other deposits, including material carried to the sea by rivers.

In the deep water of the Doldrums and other calm tropical regions this nutrient sediment sinks to the cold dark ocean abyss. Where there is no turbulence to cause an upwelling of the rich silt, organic production at the surface is starved. Numerous observations and counts of marine organisms, including sea birds, in all latitudes of the oceans, show that the still, deep, clear, very blue and very salt water found in such regions is least rich in bird life. In cruises across the equator in the three major oceans, I have known whole days to pass without a bird being seen, despite long hours of studying the calm blue water. Only in the vicinity of isolated oceanic islands do sea birds appear in any number in the tropical zone away from the continental shelf, and many of these prove to be littoral, not truly pelagic, species. The surface waters of the Antarctic are about five times richer in the essential nitrogenous material for planktonic growth than the waters of the equator. Charles Darwin observed that there is 'more variety of life in and about one leaf of kelp growing about the shore of Tierra del Fuego than in the whole Sargasso Sea'.

Lying north of the equator, but within the calm tropical zone, the Sargasso is bounded on the south by the north equatorial current as this sweeps westward to the West Indies and the Gulf of Mexico, and on the north by the same current as it emerges therefrom and flows north-east as the west-wind-drift (Figure 1).

There are similar but perhaps less well-known centres of calm sun-heated water bounded by ocean currents in the south Atlantic, the north and south Pacific and the Indian oceans where the surface is comparatively sterile, little visited by birds or larger marine life except on passage. Like the deserts of the land they produce little food, or shelter from the sun's burning heat, and are just as effective a barrier to the distribution of the more sedentary species.

The physical properties (hydrology and meteorology) of the oceans are thus as important in determining the numbers and presence of marine life as are the physical properties (geography and weather) of the land in governing the distribution of life ashore. Although the ocean is apparently flat and superficially featureless, in reality it is full of such physical barriers, mostly invisible to man, beyond which marine species pass only at mortal peril to their existence. The experienced sailor may visually detect these barriers, which lie principally at the convergence of ocean currents where the cool green turbulence of upwelling water rich in nutrients is replaced by the sterile blue of still seas. The scientist defines the zones more precisely in terms of temperature and salinity of the surface water, but as these fluctuate seasonally the limits of each zone are not perfectly static.

Because of these barriers and the attachment of each species to the special type and temperature of surface water on which it depends for food we can conveniently divide the ocean into 'zones' of marine environment for the purpose of describing their birds.

THE ANTARCTIC ZONE (Figure 2)

This extends from the antarctic continent north to the point of convergence (at around 50°S) of the layers of cool and warm currents in the southern oceans. At its southern limit the water temperature near and under the sea-ice is at freezing point, rising to barely 3·5°C at the northern edge. Due to the summer melting of pack ice and the heavy precipitation of snow and rain (more than 1,000mm annually), the salinity close to the land is low. The result of this accession of fresh water, aided by the incessant 'pull' of westerly gales to the north, is a flow of cold surface water away from Antarctica in a north-easterly direction. This movement assists the distribution and aeration of surface water which is extremely rich in nutrients, especially phosphate and nitrogen. The oxygen and hydrogen content of the sea here is higher than in any other ocean. Despite the cold, planktonic foods—diatoms, krill (shrimp-like crustaceans)—are extremely abundant, providing basic nourishment for squid, fish, and some birds, and so in turn for larger fish and birds, seals and whales.

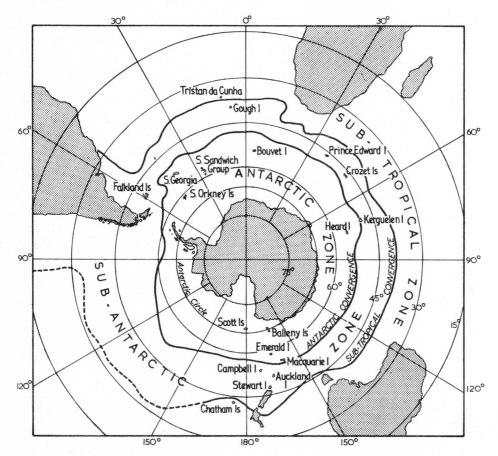

Figure 2 Zones of surface water, and their convergences, in south-polar projection

The limits of this low-temperature zone are variable around 50°S because of the projection to 55°S of the South American continent, and of the antarctic archipelago (and the Scotic Arc) north to 60°S. The warmer water of the Brazilian Current, extending its influence almost to Cape Horn, produces a higher temperature along the eastern side of that vast capeland, resulting in a climate in which forests grow farthest south in the world—in Tierra del Fuego. But a little farther east, in the same latitude as the Horn, South Georgia, bathed in polar currents, is essentially an antarctic island, treeless and mostly clothed in snow and glaciers. Other islands close to the 50°S parallel, such as Bouvet, Heard and South Orkneys, which lie unprotected in this easterly drift of polar water, are also chill treeless places, but occupied in summer by thousands of sea birds typical of the Antarctic and sub-antarctic.

BIRDS OF THE ANTARCTIC LANDS AND ICE

The birds which breed on the vast antarctic continent, its wide ice shelf and its adjacent small islands (which for most of the year remain attached to the land by bridges of sea ice), are necessarily species which obtain their living from the sea nearby, or are partly parasitic on other antarctic birds. For this frozen land produces no substantial terrestrial plant or insect food during the few weeks when part of its outer edge is free of ice. Here and there, especially on the offshore islands, grow patches of moss which, in centuries, may form quite thick layers of peat. But the rim of the continent itself, the fringe best known to exploring man, is too exposed to ice action to support other vegetative growth, save a little lichen (*Usnea* species).

During the four months November to February this edge of Antarctica and its islands experiences a short dry summer with long spells of sunshine. There is virtually no spring or autumn; the shade temperature rarely or never rises above freezing. But in the sunlight ice melts and there is intense activity among small groups and large colonies of nesting sea birds. These are few enough in species, and quickly listed. Penguins, of course, are the birds par excellence of the Antarctic; without their densely packed large colonies, their amusing fearless behaviour, to say nothing of their curiosity in the presence of man, that region would seem more desolate and inhospitable than ever.

Thirteen species of birds breed on the antarctic continent and islets joined to it by winter ice: five are penguins and six are petrels.

Emperor penguin *Aptenodytes forsteri*
King penguin *Aptenodytes patagonica*
Adelie penguin *Pygosceli adeliae*
Chinstrap penguin *Pygosceli antarctica*
Gentoo penguin *Pygosceli papua*
Giant petrel *Macronectes giganteus*
Cape pigeon *Daption capensis*
Antarctic petrel *Thalassoica antarctica*
Antarctic fulmar *Fulmarus glacialoides*
Snow petrel *Pagodroma nivea*
Wilson's storm petrel *Oceanites oceanicus*
South polar skua *Catheracta maccormicki*
Sheathbill *Chionis alba*

The lives of these polar birds are described later in the sections on penguins, petrels and skuas. Only some penguins, the snow petrel and the sheathbill remain more or less within sight of the ice all the year, feeding on euphausid shrimps. The movements of some of the penguins when not breeding are not yet fully known; the two largest, the emperor and king penguins, actually rear their single chick during the bitter temperatures and darkness of the antarctic winter. The beautiful pure-white snow petrel is not an ocean wanderer, and does not travel far from the pack ice at any time.

The sheathbill, a scavenger, the only bird without webbed feet on the antarctic continent, ranges farther north, and in winter has been seen 400 miles from the nearest coast, but generally well south of warmer subtropical water. This pure-white bird with pink eyes and yellow cheeks, pigeon-like in appearance and gait, seems to belong to no recognised family, but may be nearer the waders than the gulls. Known to whalers as 'paddy', it is a great opportunist and has been found wintering gregariously along the antarctic coast where offal and other refuse are available from the living quarters of observer and whaling stations. In September it attends the whelping grounds of the Weddell seals on the ice, and in October and November scavenges the penguin colonies for what it may snatch—eggs, young, carcases and droppings. It also eats algae and associated organisms of the tidal zone. It is impudently tame, almost walking into huts and tents, and pattering about upon the backs of resting seals. The nest is partly hidden among rock debris, and decorated with the refuse from its food: feathers, bones, shells. Here it lays two or three eggs at intervals of several days, beginning incubation with the first egg—as in all polar species this is an insurance against loss from freezing. Only one chick is reared; the laying of the second and third eggs also seems to be a form of insurance in case the first is lost. The first-hatched chick gets all the attention, and the other one, or two, disappear, probably eaten—cannibalised—before or soon after hatching. The parents are devoted to their one child, however, and feed and care for it assiduously. Late in February the young sheathbill leaves the nest site and begins a wandering life for the next two or three years before settling to a more sedentary existence on achieving a mate and breeding territory in its antarctic home.

THE SUB-ANTARCTIC ZONE (Figure 2)

The point of convergence of the layers of cool and warm currents in the southern oceans occurs first close to the shallow antarctic drift ice where near-freezing water sinks down the inshore slope to flow north under the warmer layer moving south from the open sea. This warmer water rises to a surface disturbed by the strong winds of latitude 50°S. Here the mean surface temperature is 3°C, and its turbulence is known as the Antarctic Convergence. It is very rich in the pink-coloured shrimps or krill (*Euphausia*) feeding on the abundant diatoms of the phytoplankton; and so, as already described, providing nourishment for fish and squid, swimming penguins, flying sea birds, seals and whales. Farther north the cool surface water flowing from the Antarctic Convergence, assisted by the fierce gales of the west-wind-drift, produces a stronger current in an easterly and north-easterly direction. This region, approximately between 40°S and 50°S, known as the sub-antarctic zone, has a surface temperature between 3°C and 11·5°C in winter, and from 5·5°C to 14·5°C in summer. The line of this convergence is sharply defined where the heavy antarctic surface water meets the lighter saline water of the sub-antarctic and sinks below it.

The slower rate of growth of phytoplankton and krill, and their much longer life in cooler water is another reason for the abundance of basic sea food. In warm tropical waters the lives of many invertebrates are measured in hours rather than days. Another difference is that in water constantly heated by the sun there is a greater secretion of calcium carbonate by such animals as corals, lamellibranch and gastero-pod molluscs; very little lime is secreted by related invertebrates in chilly polar seas, where they are often without shells at all.

At the limits of the sub-antarctic zone around 40°S enormous masses of the crustacean *Munida*, known to the whale fishermen as whalefeed, and to other observers as lobster-krill from its appearance, sometimes give this warmer sea a scarlet tinge. Thus we find the surface waters of the southern oceans, extending from the edge of Antarctica and its ice-shelf as far north as the roaring forties, with extensions of cold water sweeping far north along the south-west coasts of America and Africa, richest of all oceanic zones in basic plankton and crustacean life, and supporting the greatest concentrations of sea birds, seals and whales in the world.

BIRDS OF THE SUB-ANTARCTIC ZONE

As this zone extends from the Antarctic Convergence to the line of the Sub-tropical Convergence, with extensions of its cold water north against the west coasts of the southern continents (including the South Island of New Zealand), its list of characteristic sea birds is a long one. This is the true home of most of the penguins and albatrosses, and of a formidable number of petrels and shearwaters. Of these the giant petrel ranges the whole of the zone, as marking of individuals has shown, indicating a wind-drifted migration around the antarctic continent before the gales of the roaring forties. Even more ubiquitous is the cape pigeon, another circumpolar petrel which also wanders far north on the cool diversions of antarctic currents towards the equator. Wide-ranging too, but less numerous, is the delicately coloured blue petrel *Halobaena caerulea*, barely 12in (300mm) in length. Still smaller are the grey-blue whalebirds or prions, typical cool-water birds which are difficult to separate into their species at sea. Known to science as *Pachyptila* petrels, they have been divided into six or more species. They have bills differing in width and size, but all adapted for scooping up small prey at the surface and straining the water therefrom, very much as the baleen whales do, through a comb-like process along the edges of the mandibles. Most of the prions are comparatively local and sedentary, which explains why they have speciated and subspeciated in isolation—to the confusion of field and museum workers.

Over twenty of those medium-sized petrels with long wings and gliding flight, the shearwaters (*Puffinus*, *Procellaria* and *Pterodroma* species), are found in this zone. The smallest petrels, which feed by fluttering over the surface and are known as storm petrels (family *Hydrobatidae*), have four typical representatives breeding: Wilson's petrel, one of the most numerous of sea birds in the world; and the grey-backed, black-bellied and white-faced storm petrels. Almost as small as the storm-petrels, but distinct in their habits, the diving petrels *Pelecanoides* feed in a specialised way, by an underwater pursuit of their prey; they fly very little, with a heavy bee-

like whirring of the wings close to the surface. In these habits they closely resemble the auks of the northern hemisphere—an interesting case of parallel evolution from totally dissimilar ancestors. Strictly speaking they are not ocean wanderers: the four species are local and resident, confined to the sub-antarctic zone.

Wilson's storm petrels

Lastly there are the several resident southern-hemisphere cormorants or shags, a few resident species of gulls and terns, and two skuas which breed in the zone. Of these only the smaller antarctic skua (the south polar skua mentioned in the list of breeders in Antarctica) is a true ocean wanderer, crossing the equator on a winter journey thousands of miles from home. Of all the birds of the world this skua has been seen flying nearest to the South Pole.

Only one tern is both antarctic and sub-antarctic, breeding as far north as the Snares Island south of New Zealand. But it is almost sedentary, unlike its northern cousin the arctic tern which performs the longest migration of any bird (measured in a straight line) between breeding and winter range, reaching antarctic seas during the austral summer (page 144).

THE SOUTHERN SUBTROPICAL ZONE (Figure 2)

Approximately from 40°S to the Tropic of Capricorn (23° 27′ S), with considerable seasonal variation, more northerly of course in the southern winter. The surface temperature varies from 15°C at the Sub-Tropical Convergence to 23°C at the Tropical Convergence; salinity rises with temperature, while oxygen and diatom content decrease by as much as 50 per cent nearest the equator. The fast-moving Humboldt Current sweeps its cool waters well above Capricorn in the Pacific, along the west coast of South America until, north of Chile, it is known as the Peru Current. The related cold Benguela Current which brings water of antarctic origin to the west coast of South Africa likewise travels north, lowering the temperature there far north of Capricorn, so that the island of St Helena lies in a cooler, subtropical, sea; but Ascension, 800 miles to the north-west, is considered to be a fully tropical island. As it is almost impossible to fit these two cool currents into a latitudinal scheme of ocean zones, they are considered separately here.

THE HUMBOLDT CURRENT (Figure 3)

Figure 3   Diagram to show the course of the principal current movements named in the text

At the end of the austral winter the water temperature of the Humboldt-Peru Current has dropped to 17°C, even at the equator, close to the coast of Ecuador, before it turns west to bathe the Galapagos Islands in waters a few degrees warmer. It is not surprising therefore to find southern, even sub-antarctic, species including

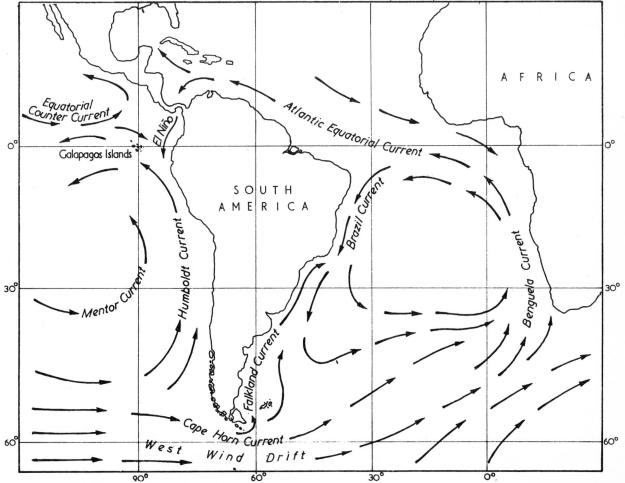

one penguin and an albatross, breeding at the Galapagos. The route by which they arrived and settled here is obvious—the strong north-going current is rich with euphausid food and fish, notably the anchovy shoals, supporting millions of sea birds. Three species of the black and white *Spheniscus* penguins nicely illustrate the principle of ecological isolation between closely related species coexisting along this South American coast. The largest is *S. magellanicus* (710mm long), breeding from Cape Horn north to Patagonia. *S. humboldti*, a little smaller, is the representative on the west side, from Valparaiso to the Peruvian coast. The smallest (510mm) is the Galapagos penguin *S. mendiculus*, perhaps the least thriving, since it suffers severe losses when the cool Humboldt waters are occasionally replaced by a sudden flow of the barren tropical El Nino Current from the north; its present numbers are estimated at about 2,000 in total.

Albatrosses are usually associated with stormy winds which give them the lift they need for their gliding flight; they are numerous as visitors to the cool breezy latitudes of the Humboldt Current off the Chilean coast. Unlike the Galapagos penguin, the Galapagos *Diomedea irrorata* (the waved albatross) can fly with ease, hundreds of miles south to fish in the cold current when the warm sterile El Nino visits the region of its only known breeding place, Hood Island in the Galapagos, where some 12,000 pairs nest.

In Chapter 6, man's exploitation of the enormous colonies of more sedentary sea birds—cormorants, boobies and pelicans—which nest on the chain of small islands off the Peruvian coast will be described, although these species are not really ocean wanderers. But they form the bulk of the sea birds enjoying the vast harvest of the main Humboldt Current feeding grounds. In the northern winter these residents are joined by great numbers of marine birds from arctic and sub-arctic shores, which feed and fatten throughout the austral summer before returning north to breed once more. These considerable travellers include skuas, gulls, terns and phalaropes, described in later chapters.

THE BENGUELA CURRENT (Figure 3)

Like its Pacific counterpart, this is a north-moving current of cool water from the south, coldest nearest the land, where it is shallowest and most subject to upwelling turbulence which brings to the surface the nutrients feeding its rich diatomic and crustacean life. Like the Humboldt, the Benguela Current is fertile and green only for a hundred miles or so offshore. Westwards in both oceans above the Southern Tropic (Capricorn) the sea becomes calmer, blue and with little life on the surface. Interestingly the Benguela Current supports, close inshore to the Cape Province, a typical *Spheniscus* penguin, a close relative of the Humboldt penguins, and so alike that a common, comparatively recent southern origin is obvious. *S. demersus* has the same piebald appearance, but is certainly a distinct species, about 630mm in length, and notable for its loud braying call from which it was named the jackass penguin. But despite the fact that they are strictly protected and breed more than once in the year, laying eggs in spring (September) and again in autumn (February), they have decreased. Recently the closing of the Suez Canal and the re-routing of large oil tankers from the Persian Gulf around the Cape of Good Hope has presented this penguin, among other sea birds, with a new danger: it has suffered severely as the result of discharge of crude oil off that coast.

The Cape gannet *Sula capensis* is an inhabitant of the fertile Benguela stream. Unique to South Africa, it differs little in appearance and habits from the North Atlantic *S. bassana*. Migrating north along the Benguela Current in winter it may reach the equator at a time when the northern gannet has flown therefrom, to its breeding islets beyond 50°N. Accompanying the Cape gannet on its winter voyage towards the equator and back is the Damara tern *Sterna balaenarum*, nesting in South Africa. There are many other migratory as well as less pelagic birds to be seen moving past the Cape of Good Hope; I have counted thousands in a day spent at this southern extremity of Africa. For its western side, bathed by the cold water from south, is a rich feeding ground as well as a flyway for both northern and southern breeding birds. I saw albatrosses from the south at the same moment as terns and phalaropes from the north. Immature or otherwise unoccupied migrant sea birds, with no urge to breed, may remain for over a year in winter quarters, in both the Benguela and the Humboldt Currents, so that some antarctic and sub-antarctic albatrosses, petrels, shearwaters, terns and skuas mingle there with northern-hemisphere petrels, shearwaters, terns, skuas and waders.

INDIAN OCEAN CURRENTS (Figure 1)

The cool west-wind current drifts along the southern Indian Ocean and the south coast of Australia without hindrance of land as far as Tasmania. The warm counter (equatorial) current of this ocean is diverted anticlockwise south around Madagascar to meet the cold Benguela water at the Cape of Good Hope. People at Cape Town have the choice of bathing in waters of very different temperatures: on the Atlantic side the chilly surf of the Benguela, on the east side the warmer billows of the Mozambique Current. South-east trade winds blow fairly constantly all the year in mid-Indian Ocean; but in the northern area, between the equator and the Tropic of Cancer there are seasonal monsoon winds, carrying heavy rain, north-easterly in direction in winter, south-westerly in summer, which affect surface movements of the water. Here sea-surface temperatures are as high (28°C) as in equatorial Pacific and Atlantic waters. There are long intervals of calm however, when the heated sea would be barren of sea bird life if small areas of local upwelling did not occur, bringing to the surface water as cool as 14°C, colder indeed than the Humboldt Current in a comparable latitude. Off Somalia an extremely swift current, nearly 7 knots at times, flows south-west across the equator in the northern winter and, impelled by the south-west monsoon, in the opposite direction in the northern summer. Certain sea birds concentrate in this zone of upwelling which is determined by two factors: the underlying topography of the ocean floor, and the flow of the wind-driven currents at the surface, dragging the cold abyssal water upwards.

Typical pelagic sea birds of the Indian Ocean north of the Southern Tropic include Wilson's petrel (which in the austral winter covers the whole ocean and enters the Red Sea and the Persian Gulf), several shearwaters, one or more *Fregatta* petrels, terns, tropic birds, boobies, and phalaropes.

THE TROPICAL ZONE, PACIFIC AND ATLANTIC OCEANS (Figure 1)

This extends as described earlier, between the tropics of Cancer and Capricorn, with variable limits, depending on cold currents. The surface temperature may rise to 29°C, with the greatest salinity in the centre, due to low rainfall and high evaporation under almost continuous anti-cyclonic conditions, very calm and, away from the continents, with few islands to attract nesting sea birds. Tropic birds, *Phaeton* species, are characteristic of these sea deserts, briefly visiting passing ships, a habit which has earned them the sailor's name of bo'sun bird from the shrill call, and the long tail which resembles a boatswain's marlinspike. Otherwise the voyager will see only a few petrels, shearwaters, skuas and terns making their way north or south on their transequatorial migrations. But nearer the few islands there will be boobies and frigate birds and certain tropical breeding petrels, shearwaters and terns. Some equatorial breeders are of worldwide (pan-tropical) distribution, such as the Madeiran petrel *Oceanodroma castro*, and Audubon's shearwater *Puffinus l'hermniieri*, two birds which have nevertheless been divided into regional sub-species, with slight anatomical differences, by some taxonomists. Breeding far apart on remote islands, and keeping to limited feeding zones within a few hundred miles of their nesting burrows, groups of these and other tropical and subtropical petrels form largely self-contained, genetically closed, communities; they are subspecies, if not species in the making, but almost impossible to distinguish as such in the open sea.

Sooty and noddy terns range over most areas of tropical and subtropical seas; and their lives are described in the chapter on terns.

THE NORTHERN SUBTROPICAL ZONE (Figure 1)

Subject to the same influences of winds (or lack of) as its southern counterpart (but in a reverse, clockwise direction), of the effects of depth of water, of salinity (locally increased by evaporation and decreased by river dilution), the northern subtropical zone has similar ranges of surface temperature, approximately between 18°C and 25°C. These remarks apply only to the Pacific and Atlantic: there is of course no northern subtropical zone in the Indian Ocean.

In the land-locked North Pacific this zone is less complicated than in the smaller North Atlantic with its wide north-eastern outlet to the Arctic Ocean. In both oceans the clockwise winds and currents circle the calm centre, warmer in the western half of both, where Sargasso-type dead water is encountered. A cold current reaches far down to California on the east side of the Pacific, a flyway and feeding ground of northern and arctic migrants. In mid-ocean the Hawaiian Islands chain has two breeding albatrosses, the black-footed *Diomedea nigripes*, and the Laysan *D. immutabilis*; and the rarest albatross in the world survives only on the Japanese island of Toroshima, the short-tailed *D. albatrus*. Recent oceanographical surveys for the Smithsonian Institution during 15 months' cruise along a replicate track of a total of 34,384 nautical miles (63,610km) to the east, north and south of the Hawaiian Islands yielded 13,080 sightings of 65,707 birds (King, 1970)—rather surprisingly for this fairly calm region. This list of ocean-going birds recorded in mid-north Pacific is formidable: some 20 species of shearwater and gadfly petrels, 4 or more of storm petrels, 2 tropic birds, 3 boobies, the great frigate bird; and skuas, gulls, terns, waders and phalaropes.

In the same zone of the Atlantic there are fewer islands: the Canaries, Azores and Madeira in the east, Bermuda and the northern Bahamas in the west; and there

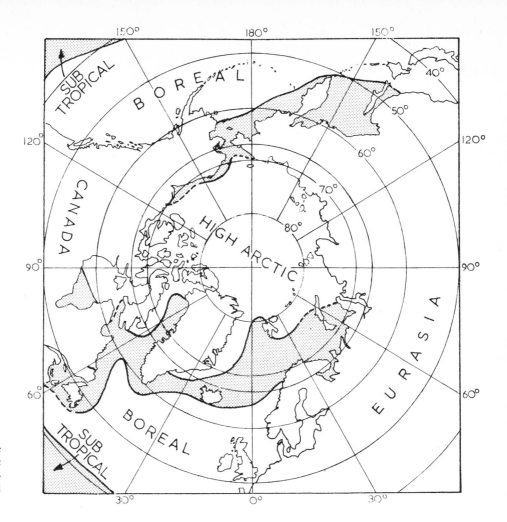

Figure 4 Zones of marine environment. High Arctic and Boreal unshaded; Sub-Arctic and Sub-tropical shaded

are rather fewer representatives of these families, as breeders or pelagic visitors.

BOREAL ZONE (Figure 4)

This is a distinct zone of marine environment, approximately north of latitude 40°N, which some oceanographers insert as a buffer zone between the subtropical and sub-arctic water. As a result of its strong winds, turbulent currents and high tides its waters provide some of the richest fisheries in the world, now much over-exploited as a food source for the millions of people inhabiting its seaboard of western Europe, temperate North America, and Japan.

This boreal zone in both oceans supports large breeding populations of gulls, terns, auks, shearwaters and petrels; but the northern-hemisphere gannet is confined to breeding colonies in small islands off north-western Europe and the Gulf of St Lawrence (Figure 6, page 76).

THE SUB-ARCTIC ZONE (Figure 4)

The water-surface temperature corresponds to that of the sub-antarctic zone, from about 3°C to 11·5°C in winter; and up to 14·5°C in summer, when the isothermic line moves north very unevenly, as shown in Figure 4. July is the height of the arctic

65

summer, when thousands of sea birds, geese, ducks and waders are hatching eggs and rearing young on cliffs, low shores, windswept islands and islets, and on the treeless tundra of low-arctic Eurasia and North America. According to Sverdrup, arctic waters have 23 species of holoplanktonic animals compared with 71 species in the Antarctic, with 11 species common to both. However the numbers of individuals of edible species, rather than the number of species, is more important to the birds and other animals which rely on plankton as the base of the food chain. In summer, low and high arctic waters swarm with a reddish planktonic 'bloom'.

The sub-arctic zone supports at least sixty breeding sea birds, including both littoral and oceanic species; some of these also breed farther north and others farther south, with some subspecific differences indicating genetically closed communities. A number of southern-hemisphere breeders wander into boreal and low-arctic seas during the northern summer, to feed on its rich food supply while they are moulting—and incidentally escaping the rigours of the austral winter.

Auks are typical of this and the next zone.

THE HIGH ARCTIC (Figure 4)

Surface temperature, even in summer, is $-1°C$ close to the pack ice, and rarely rises above $5°C$. The ice-laden current which pours through the narrows of Bering Strait lowers the water temperature around the Aleutian chain at all seasons, and in mid-winter well below freezing point; and westwards the winter ice blocks east Asian harbours south to $50°S$, as does the ice of the Labrador current along the shores of eastern Canada in the Atlantic. Some land birds survive the high-arctic winter above $70°N$, such as the resident ptarmigan, but no pelagic sea birds remain. The beautiful pure-white ivory gull *Pagophila eburnea* is resident, however, and must be the hardiest bird in the northern hemisphere, since it normally remains within the shores of the polar basin, finding food even in winter from arctic shrimps picked up in 'leads' of open water, and from the droppings and carcases of seal, walrus and polar bear. Few have seen this gull in breeding plumage; but occasionally immatures in greyer feather wander south into the Atlantic.

The handsome Sabine's gull *Xema sabini* makes an extended migration south across the equator, to appear off the coasts of Peru and Chile in some numbers; and smaller flocks visit the south Atlantic.

One of the rarest gulls is the rosy or Ross's gull *Rhodostethia rosea*; for years its breeding grounds were unknown. It mysteriously appeared on the north coast of Alaska in autumn *heading east* towards the increasing ice sheet and frozen Canadian arctic archipelago. Eventually it was proved to breed in the deltas of eastern Siberia. It strays but rarely from the pack ice.

Even in summer the truly arctic-breeding sea birds are few in species, though often extremely abundant in numbers of individuals. Only one petrel is high-arctic, the fulmar (Figure 7). But the auks are typical and well represented, although they do not make very long migrations, content to reach ice-free sea in winter.

Record long-distance traveller of all birds is the arctic tern *Sterna paradisaea* which, breeding on high and low arctic and boreal zone shores, reaches the pack ice of the Antarctic in the southern summer and, as described later, evidently circles the South Polar continent during its 'winter' sojourn there. Thus among all living organisms it experiences the most daylight during the year.

5 EXPERT NAVIGATORS

It is fascinating to speculate on how and when migration was extended in some birds which today make an annual voyage of several thousand miles across the equator between their far-north breeding grounds and their far-south wintering region, and vice versa. More than two-thirds of their lives are thereby spent in the northern and southern summers, with only a few weeks of migration across the equatorial region, spring and autumn.

More remarkable still is the ability of the young bird, on leaving the nest, to make its first long migration alone. Most of the evidence we have, through direct observation and from marking of nestlings, indicates that, although adult and immature birds freely move in mixed flocks at sea, many fledglings at first migrate alone, some leaving the nest several days after the adults have vanished; but yet these lone young birds arrive quickly at the traditional wintering area, thousands of miles distant. How is this possible?

From the discussion in the first chapter we may suppose that migrations from high latitudes in autumn, and towards the poles in spring, was originally induced by pressures of population and food-seeking during the advance and retreat of the ice caps over tens of thousands of years. This movement became part of the annual cycle of those birds which were able to feed and breed in the persistent daylight and fertile seas of northern and southern polar summers, but where winter is a long dark night with weather too severe to support or enable the gathering of an adequate food supply. (The exceptions, unique among sea birds, are the two largest penguins, rearing their chicks in winter on the antarctic ice, as described later in this book.)

Some birds migrate in flocks, adults and young together; in these species the young birds have the possible advantage of learning the route by following their parents. But in these gregarious migrants is the individual youngster, accidentally delayed and unable to keep up with the adults, able to find the way quite alone? A long delay might be fatal, since it is known that in many long-distance migrants the urge to travel does not last more than a few weeks: the impulse is very strong at the traditional moment, causing restlessness in a caged bird, but it is only one link in the seasonal rhythm or cycle of activity in the migrant's year, and once that rhythm is broken its chances of survival are reduced. However, some interesting tests have been made to show that, in some social migrants, even the guidance of experienced adults is not essential. Young crows were raised in captivity in Alberta, Canada, and released long after the wild crows had flown south to normal winter quarters in Oklahoma. When the artificially reared crows were set free they took off rapidly, and flew in the direction of Oklahoma, some being shot along the route to prove this. These crows were born with an innate sense of their geographical position in relation to the normal migration route of their species, which enabled them to follow that route to winter quarters they had never seen before.

Certain swans, geese and ducks migrate over considerable distances in family parties, keeping together as a unit until and often long after they have reached the wintering area. But although this guidance by the adults which lead the formation through the sky may be useful to the youngsters making their first migration, it is probably incidental to the established habit of family togetherness, a behavioural trait of some survival and protective value. In another test, 1,271 juvenile blue-winged teal banded on their autumn migration through Illinois, were kept in captivity until long after all other ducks had flown south; after release 111 were subsequently shot along their true migration route south-eastwards, a normal percentage loss from gunners. So these young ducks too 'knew' the correct direction instinctively.

There is now strong evidence that the bird possesses the equivalent of the human navigator's aids; but in the form of a complicated mechanism in its brain which is genetically programmed with innate information, and able to respond to external and internal stimuli so as to guide the bird accurately along traditional flyways it has not learned by example. In making its first migration alone the young bird, however, receives impressions of the sun and star patterns along the route, and evidently retains these as visual memories for future guidance.

For its chronometer the bird has an accurate time-sense, by which it appears to be aware not only of the hours of the day and night, but also of the days and months when it will mate, breed and migrate—that is, of the seasons. Many animals in fact have this acute sense of time, although in sophisticated man it is largely atrophied. The physical nature and working of the bird's biological clock is not by any means fully understood; but light in varying intensity from sun, stars, moon, planets and their exact observed position in the heavens is received through the bird's eye, by electric impulse reaches the brain, as in man and other animals, and is fed to the memory cells: either to the untested inherited memory of the young bird, or to the stored visual memories of the experienced traveller. This initiates appropriate action to keep a true course. In effect the bird appears to carry in its brain a chronometer, a form of sextant, and the essential charts for the traditional migration passage.

That the migrant reads the positions of the heavenly bodies at any moment they are visible, so assessing its longitude (=local time) and latitude, albeit instinctively and without intelligent calculation, seems proved by the fact that in heavily overcast weather, mist or fog, with the celestial signs invisible, it invariably ceases to migrate; or if it continues to move about then, it appears to be disoriented, strays from the true course, or circles aimlessly. Once the sky clears it is able to re-orientate correctly, even if displaced from the proper route in the interval. Migrants blown by strong winds far off course are able to return to the traditional flyway—under a clear sky. Some birds will rise above fog and dense cloud like a long-distance plane. But sea birds almost invariably migrate low over the sea. It has not been proved that migrating birds receive guidance from external electrical phenomena or the earth's magnetic forces; if they did they would not be lost in a fog. They do not carry a magnetic compass; but they may recognise, and in the northern hemisphere be guided by, the North Star (Polaris), from its brightness and unchanging position, with the other major stars wheeling westwards around it in a fixed pattern. In the southern hemisphere the Southern Cross with its associated fixed stars could be a similar guide. It is not possible of course to allow that migrants deliberately study the positions of the stars, and consciously compute the traditional route. But we know that their innate rhythms of migration, moult and reproduction are timed with great exactness, each phase often commencing on the same date year after year. Internally this timing is controlled by the mysterious computer in the brain, linked with the hypothalmus, anterior pituitary gland and gonads, through the highly sensitive eye. But its punctuality means that year after year the migrant is on passage over the same part of the traditional route on or about the same day or night. Hence it recognises, and is the more easily guided by, the regular (apparent) annual movements of the fixed stars, or of the sun. It is argued that those set patterns which recur during the precise few hours of the day or night when the bird is migrating along its regular flyway in spring or autumn have become fixed in the genetic memory during aeons of evolutionary pressures selecting those migrants which exploited successfully the advantages of following the sun into spring in both hemispheres. (The apparent courses of the sun and the major fixed stars at any given hour in the year alter so slowly in the heavens that they remain sufficiently static during each epoch for man's navigational calculations. Any gradual alteration takes a century of time, during which the change could be registered in the genetic computer carried in the heads of the many generations of birds living through that epoch.)

Unfortunately for this theory of astral navigation, while the sun and fixed stars are constant in time and position at each given moment of the year, as viewed from any point on earth, the moon and the planets are not. The bright light and erratic movements of these bodies must surely influence and even confuse the light-sensitive computer of the bird navigating by the fixed stars at night? And much migration, at least of land birds, has been observed across the face of the moon by night-watching ornithologists. But here we are concerned with oceanic birds, the majority of which appear to migrate by day, and rest by night (some have been observed feeding during moonlit periods when many species of fish, crustaceans and squid rise to the surface).

The short answer to the riddle of bird navigation and orientation is that no one has yet discovered, despite many homing and other tests with marked individuals, by what *physical* process the young bird is able to navigate alone over great distances with such accuracy in place and time; but the evidence is for some form of guidance from the sky, so long as this is not totally obscured by cloud or mist. Obviously too, sea birds observe much that is important of what they see below: the waves and currents of the ocean, the outlines of lands and islands, isolated rocks— of which the youngster will retain visual memories, beginning with the nest site and place where it was reared, and to which it will one day return to breed.

Once it has made the initial 'instinctive' voyage from its birth place to winter quarters, the migrant may be said to be visually imprinted with the physical topography of sky, earth and sea, replacing or augmenting its inherited knowledge of the route. It has now 'learned' the way, and in doing so has had many other experiences useful for its survival: encounters with enemies, with bad weather, with neutral birds, with adults of its own species; and has, from its natural appetite, learned how to find adequate food.

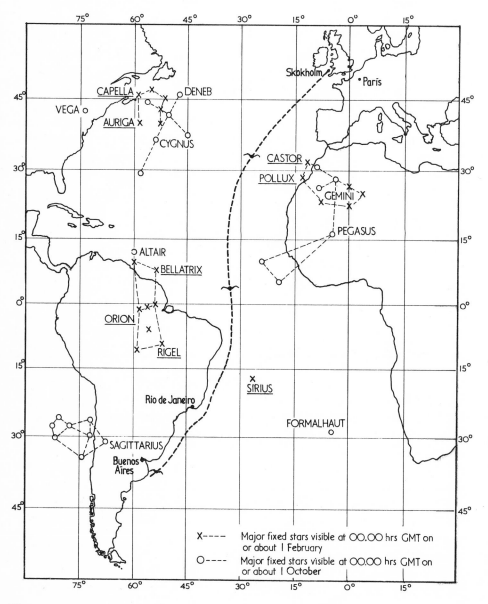

Figure 5 The approximate positions of the major stars as seen at midnight above a shearwater on its annual migration of several thousand miles between Skokholm, its nesting island in Wales, and its wintering grounds off the coasts of Brazil and the Argentine. The major fixed stars visible at 00.00 hours GMT on or about 1 February on the spring migration northwards are underlined. The major stars visible at 00.00 hours on or about 1 October during the autumn migration southwards are not underlined

The importance and strength of this first imprinting or visual impression of its birthplace on the newly born has been demonstrated by many experiments with various animals such as migratory salmon: these and other pelagic fish, whales, turtles and seals, navigate in the same way as do oceanic birds, by an instinctive knowledge of the movements of the celestial bodies, or at least of the sun, across the sky during the hours of their migrations. Even if they swam little at the surface, the angle of the sun's light could be observed at some distance below, and in conjunction with their exact biological chronometer would give them their world position.

The young migrant does not necessarily retrace its outward flight on its return home. And here is another remarkable facet of its inherited memory: in several species of pelagic sea birds the whole migration to and from winter quarters, particularly of the immatures or non-breeders, is in the form of an ellipse, even a figure-of-eight (see Figures 12 to 13), covering new areas of ocean almost all the way. Moreover, one or more years may elapse before the young bird is mature enough to respond to the sexual drive to set up nesting territory, find a mate and breed. Long after the adults, established breeders of previous seasons, have returned to the nesting ground, the young bird fledged in the previous season may linger in or near the wintering region at sea, may indeed spend the whole summer on the farther side of the equator. Yet its visual memory of the position and physical features of its birthplace has been retained and in due course will enable it to recognise the site; this despite the fact that on its first return voyage it will not be piloted by the adults, which by then are already nesting far away. Its first landing at or near its birthplace will be later in the summer and often by a different, more leisurely approach, taking the other arm of the elliptical or figure-of-eight movement, migrating homewards by a traverse it has never made before.

In some sea birds, notably albatrosses, the immature period of wandering the oceans by established routes and feeding grounds may last more than one year, and up to eight years, before successful breeding takes place; but usually these adolescents will make a close approach to the breeding ground before then, although even so may not land. They are so to speak 'keeping an eye open', refreshing their memory of the breeding range against the day when the sexual drive impels them to go ashore in their first, usually unsuccessful, exploration in search of territory and a mate, long after the adults have started nesting.

Pelagic sea birds of all ages, as experiments have repeatedly shown, exhibit this marvellous sense of geographical position. But on reflection one realises that such an ability is essential in those species which traverse the featureless sea in search of their food and of summer temperatures to 'winter' in; and which are occasionally blown or drifted hundreds of miles from their normal range by severe gales. But what happens when they are released far inland?

In tests which I made with David Lack as long ago as 1937, Manx shearwaters nesting at Skokholm promptly returned to their burrows on Skokholm Island, Wales, from both sea and inland localities up to several hundred miles from home. Of these, two returned from Venice in the Adriatic, a sea which this shearwater normally never visits. It was significant that on release at Venice one shearwater, instead of flying south-east into the open Adriatic (as might be expected of such an oceanic bird which never deliberately crosses the land) and making a sea-journey of 3,700 miles through the Adriatic, Mediterranean and so via the Strait of Gibraltar to a familiar route in the Atlantic, was observed to circle up into the clear sky and head in a direct line (930 miles overland) for Skokholm, a route which would involve crossing the Italian Alps and diagonally across the whole of France. It was re-captured at its burrow on Skokholm 14 days later.

Further tests with shearwaters showed that at any inland locality in western Europe where they had been released, provided the sky was clear or only partly obscured, the majority of individuals returned rapidly, after heading in the correct direction as soon as freed. The next step was to send individuals (always with nest, mate and egg or chick to attract them home) much farther distances. Out of four Skokholm shearwaters sent by air to Boston, Massachusetts, in two separate tests, two were recovered, $12\frac{1}{2}$ and 14 days later, back at their nests. They had flown 3,050 miles, making an average of more than 200 miles each 24 hours. These releases were at the edge of Boston airport which faces the open sea—a good start for the shearwaters; once they had flown a few hundred miles eastwards they would have reached waters south of the Newfoundland Banks and north of Bermuda which would be familiar to them—at least during their early non-breeding period of leisurely summer wandering in this region of the North Atlantic.

In all these homing experiments some birds failed to return; but the tests were hampered by the human failure to maintain observation at the nest site continuously and for a sufficiently long period, so that it is probable that some successful homing birds were never recovered; and some were not recaptured until a year later.

No tests have been made, to my knowledge, by releasing pelagic sea birds, breeding in the Atlantic, in the Pacific Ocean, or vice-versa. But in the Pacific an interesting test proved that albatrosses were able to beat the homing records of the shearwaters mentioned above. When Laysan albatrosses at Midway Island

Great and sooty shearwaters from the southern hemisphere assemble to feed with fulmars on the rich fishing Grand Banks off Newfoundland

became a hazard to aeroplanes using the new military base there (see page 105), five of those which had nests on or near the new runways were transported and released 1,665 miles away; all returned. Another returned when released 2,625 miles from home; two out of four got back to Midway from 3,200 miles away (one in the record time of 10 days—around 320 miles a day); and finally one released in the Philippines flew 4,120 miles home in 32 days.

EFFECTS OF WINDS AND HURRICANES

Generally ocean-wandering birds take advantage of normal prevailing winds to assist their long migrations. Indeed the routes of these journeys almost certainly evolved through the presence and pressures of regular trade and other seasonal or permanent winds. These migrations however are not necessarily straight down the prevailing wind, which would often mean a rapid latitudinal progress (which is not the case, most migrations are longitudinal), and some loss of dynamic air-lift. They are more often at an angle to the wind, frequently less than a right angle, and are thereby subjected to drift according to the strength of the wind. For example a tern migrating and heading southwards towards Africa from its nesting site in Greenland, at its normal flight speed of 25/30 mph, if it encountered a 10 mph westerly (prevailing) wind in crossing the North Atlantic, would be drifted a calculable number of miles to the east. But, as anyone who has closely observed migration at sea will realise, the sea bird is able to compensate for drift; and in this example it would keep more or less on its true migration course—a straight (Great Circle) line for its objective of winter quarters—by flying a few degrees west of south. Progress is slower than flying downwind, but the bird heading at an angle to the wind enjoys a stronger air-lift to support it. Through its acute navigational sense it is able to make the necessary correction for wind drift; but it cannot make any headway when adverse wind speed is greater than its own flight speed. When this happens the migrant, if it does not cease flying and rest on the water (where the leeward drift will be much less), will be drifted far to one side of its course; or, if it attempts to head into the storm, directly backwards. However, sea birds are adept at taking advantage of the comparative calm to be found in the troughs between high storm-waves at sea, and will fly along these sheltered valleys, thus minimising their amount of drift to the speed of the wave, which is normally moving—a sheltering hillock of water—at right angles to the wind.

Occasionally birds encounter severe gales of up to and above 100 mph, and unless there is plenty of sea room to drift clear of the land while the hurricane lasts, they are blown ashore, and often crash-land far from the sea. Particularly vulnerable are young birds with little experience of flying, and adults in moult. Battered by the long storm and unable to feed, they live on their stores of body fat, and when these are used up, the food reserves of the muscles and vital organs keep the bird alive for a further short period—until it dies of exhaustion and starvation. From time to time 'wrecks' of sea-birds occur after such storms, and often one species is more affected than others because the cyclone struck through the wintering or migrating flock and swept it ashore. Hurricanes have very little effect on the numbers of sea birds.

6 MAN AND SEA BIRDS

Next in importance to food and living space as major factors controlling the lives of man, sea birds and all living organisms, are predators and disease. These are many and diverse, from bacteria and viruses to the most powerful animal predator of all—man himself. Barely a thousand years ago, before man multiplied to his present record population, the numbers of oceanic birds were probably much higher; but their documented history had hardly begun, and the few references to sea birds of that period are mostly unreliable, with quaint and inaccurate illustrations. Not until man succeeded in building ships large enough to cross the oceans freely do we find reasonably accurate descriptions of the birds encountered. This early history, beginning with Viking and Norman voyages, is largely a tale of hunting on remote islands and shores, and at sea: the victims were eaten, and their feathers used to stuff bedding or to clothe and adorn the human body.

Before man the colonist arrived with his lethal weapons, and his habit of introducing other predatory animals, some sea birds, especially the petrel family, nested far inland, on high mountains—presumably because the mainland cliffs were already overcrowded with other sea-bird colonies—although these birds are unable to feed except at sea. Only relict populations of the inland nesting colonies still survive here and there, in rugged and sheer terrain. The process of extermination or heavy reduction of sea-bird numbers, by man and introduced predatory animals, continued in all oceans as each island was colonised by man, right down to the beginning of the present century. It has not yet ceased; but a majority of nations now regulate the taking of sea birds—at least of those species which are regarded as useful or harmless to man. Certain small islands, usually unfit for human occupation, have been set aside as bird sanctuaries, some because of the value of the guano produced by the birds, a few purely for conservation of their fauna and flora.

If the numbers of marine birds were at a maximum in relation to their food supply when the world human population was only a few millions, that is before the advent of ocean-going peoples, a much smaller population of such birds is now exploiting what, at least theoretically, must be a more than ample food supply. Is this the case?

In general it does seem so. Where certain species have of recent years been given strict protection at their breeding stations after centuries of persecution, they have usually increased rapidly in numbers. We can cite the world population of the three species of gannet—Northern, South African and Australian; the shearwaters and petrels no longer farmed on island sanctuaries in both hemispheres; the guano-producing cormorants of western South America. Other sea birds have increased recently for other reasons (that is, without special protection), such as access to a relatively new source of food derived from human wastes; and by breeding at a site where man is no longer a predator because he has other, less laboriously obtained, sources of protein (sea-bird colonies in Iceland, the Faeroes, the Hebrides). Elsewhere the numerically flourishing species of oceanic birds today are chiefly those which breed on remote islands or coasts either protected or rarely visited by man, and in regions where the seas are still rich in their foods, unpolluted by man's industrial spillage.

SEA BIRDS AS FOOD

Man's impact on the penguin-like great auk *Alca impennis* is notorious, and well documented. Its persecution began before the existence of the true, southern-hemisphere, penguins was recorded. In the northern hemisphere, as already mentioned, a family of swimming and diving birds evolved to occupy the comparable ecological niche in cool arctic seas which the penguins enjoy in the far south: a nice example of convergent evolution in cold-water birds separated by the wide barrier of the tropics. The term penguin (from the Latin *pinguis*, fat) was first given to the great auk, and later to the true penguins, by the first sailors and explorers from Europe who had seen, or were familiar with accounts of, the great auk. As far back as Viking days the Norse raiders knew of the great auk of Iceland, and the northern isles of Scotland, and hunted and ate it along with other seafowl. When Jacques Cartier visited certain 'penguin islands' (the Funk Islands) off Newfoundland in May 1534, he and his crew filled several barrels with these large flightless 'pinguins', and salted them down for future consumption. So severe was the slaughter in the next three centuries that the great auk became extinct in its known breeding haunts, originally extending from Newfoundland, via Greenland and Iceland, to the Hebrides (Figure 6). The last one was killed at a stack rock off Iceland in 1884.

Little is known about the life of the great auk. The best account is by Martin Martin who in June 1697 arrived at remote St Kilda, farthest west of the Hebrides, as tutor to the son of the laird MacLeod. He wrote what I believe to be an accurate assessment of its breeding habits:

The Sea-Fowl are, first, *Gairfowl*, being the stateliest, as well as the largest sort, and above the Size of a *Solan Goose*, of a black Colour, red about the Eyes, a large white

75

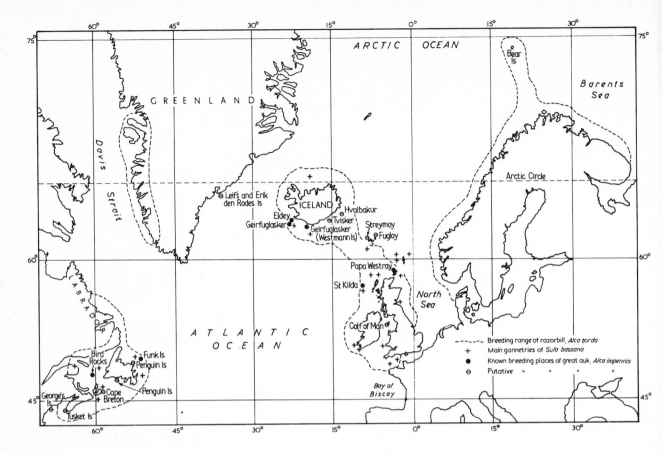

Figure 6 Known and putative breeding places of great auk *Alca impennis*, breeding range of razorbill *Alca torda* and main gannetries of *Sula bassana*

Spot under each, a long broad Bill; it stands stately, its whole Body erected, its Wings short, flies not at all; lays its Egg upon the bare Rock, which, if taken away, she lays no more for that year; she is whole footed, and has the hatching *Spot* upon her breast, *i.e.* a bare spot from which the Feathers have fallen off with the Heat in hatching; its Egg is twice as big as that of a *Solan* Goose, and is variously spotted, Black, Green, and Dark; it comes without Regard to any wind, appears the first of *May*, and goes away about the middle of June.

How the flightless great auk lived at sea we can only guess. Was it truly oceanic, a long-distance swimmer, like some migrant penguins? Certainly in order to survive it needed to swim south during the last severe glaciation of the North Atlantic. Its bones have been found in Jersey in caves of Neanderthal man (living about 20,000 years ago); also at Gibraltar, Spain, and elsewhere in the western Mediterranean, many hundreds of miles from its known breeding rocks. There is no proof that it ever bred so far south; but, significantly enough, marking of its cousin the razorbill has shown that although a poor flier on whirring stumpy wings, this too migrates, swimming much, from the same northern latitudes where the great auk once bred, and winters in the western Mediterranean.

It has been said that in any case the flightless great auk was on its way out; it had failed to adapt to its modern predator, man, just as the flightless dodo of the Indian Ocean and the moas of New Zealand failed. If only the great auk had returned, after the last glaciation, to breed as far north as the little auk now breeds—in countless thousands—on lonely Spitzbergen, Greenland, and the Canadian Arctic, it might have survived to enjoy the international protection of our present conservation-minded society. But the great auk never adapted to a sub-polar climate; it was in fact a bird of temperate seas, living in summer along the edge of the upwelling feeding zone where cool northern currents mingled with the warm west-wind-drift water, a zone eagerly exploited by the cod fishermen who raided its rookeries for fresh bird-meat.

The great auk is the sole known example of the extinction of a pelagic sea bird within the last thousand years, but one or two other oceanic species have come near to suffering the same fate. Often an advertised attraction to colonists was the multitude of edible sea birds. Even those which nested on island mountain tops, or in holes in rocks and boulders were not safe; the black or brown rats which man brought with him in his verminous wooden sailing ships (along with a less serious pest, the house mouse), were accidental colonists, but nonetheless lethal, devouring eggs and young birds, and so depriving man of this source of food. To destroy the rats and mice man introduced cats, and on some islands the mongoose. Pigs were set free on wooded and bush-covered islands, to provide food; to say nothing of other mammals such as rabbits, hares, deer, opossums and wallabies, and other food and fur-bearing animals, some of which had escaped from captivity. They multiplied, often with terrible consequences for the native avifauna. Hitherto free of terrestrial mammal predators and competitors, island birds had no adequate defence mechanism against the invaders.

On the largest island, of Australia, having introduced rabbits, man then set free cats, ferrets, stoats and weasels in an endeavour to control both rabbits and rats. He even introduced foxes, which are predators of sea birds and can wipe out whole colonies of surface-nesting penguins, terns and gulls; but, oddly, this introduction was originally for the sake of the sport of fox-hunting!

In New Zealand there were no land mammals until the first colonists, from the tropical Polynesian islands, brought with them the small Polynesian rat *Rattus exulans*, which quickly overran the New Zealand islands, but was soon exterminated on the main North and South Islands by the introduced cats, stoats, weasels, brown and black rats, and is now confined to a few offshore islets (see page 108 for its effect on nesting albatrosses and other sea birds). All these ground predators have reduced the number of burrowing birds on the main islands: the handsome owl parrot, nesting in holes, is on the verge of extinction; the little blue penguins grow scarcer every year, although the large yellow-eyed penguin is tough enough to defy these enemies; the petrels and shearwaters nesting on mountain tops and in high bush country dwindle in numbers annually.

A much older example of introduced predation upon a burrowing sea bird is the case of the diablotin or black-capped petrel *Pterodroma hasitata* of the West Indies, considered by visiting ornithologists sixty years ago to be on the point of extinction on the islands of Guadeloupe, Dominica, Martinique and Hispaniola (Haiti with San Domingo), where it formerly bred in large numbers. With the successive introduction of rats, cats, dogs and mongooses, the diablotin was forced to nest on the most inaccessible mountain cliffs.

The diablotin is a (northern) winter breeder, and those who in the past sought for it ashore in summer would have done so in vain. It returns to its wild craggy fastness in the mountains in October and departs seven months later. Breeding through the cold mountain winter may have helped to protect it from man, at least during inclement weather. Similarly its close relative, the cahow *Pterodroma*

This long-tailed skua was
determined to see that the
human intruder left its
tundra breeding site

cahow, formerly breeding in great numbers in the sea-cliffs and islets of Bermuda,
may have been saved by its winter-breeding habit. The cahow was thought to be
extinct before the middle of the seventeenth century. Following the discovery and
colonisation of Bermuda by Spain early in that century this petrel—named after its
cackling call—was by 1629 reduced from probably many thousands to nil on the
main island. Ships' crews killed the fat delicious cahow, and also the abundant
Audubon's shearwaters, drying and salting what they could not eat fresh. Introduced pigs and rats rooted and ran through the burrows of both petrels. As no
museum skins of the cahow existed it was thought that early references to this
species were mistaken and really referred to the former abundance, and subsequent
reduction, of Audubon's shearwater only. But on 20 February 1906 Louis L.
Mowbray of Bermuda found a black-capped petrel with white underparts in a

rock crevice on an islet offshore. It was unlike any other known, except that it appeared to be related to the diablotin. Ten years later Mowbray, with J. T. Nichols, named it as a true species, having unearthed a large number of its bones from the floor of cavities in the rocks where it had evidently bred for centuries. These remains were confirmed by R. W. Shufeldt as belonging to the true cahow.

Then, on 8 June 1935 a bird was brought to the research biologist William Beebe, working at that time in Bermuda: it had been picked up by a keeper at St David's lighthouse. Subsequently Murphy and Mowbray mounted an expedition to search the tiny islets and rocks off Bermuda during what was correctly suspected to be its breeding season—the northern winter. On 28 January 1951 they found a cahow incubating its egg in a 6ft long burrow on a small eroded islet; and altogether these islets were found to hold about a dozen breeding pairs. Since that year the Bermuda government has strictly protected the cahow. From the present study of the colony David Wingate reports (by letter, 1974) that there are some twenty pairs breeding under protection. One problem is to prevent the tropic bird from ousting the cahow by invading and using its burrow.

The cahow must be the world's rarest pelagic sea bird today, and little is known of where it wanders in feeding expeditions and during the five months when it is not breeding ashore. But there are others in the petrel and shearwater family whose survival is also in the balance. For instance the mid-Pacific representative of the diablotin known to science as *Pterodroma phaeopygia*, the dark-rumped petrel. Found only in the formerly mammal-less Galapagos and Hawaiian Islands, it has been drastically reduced by much the same introduced predators as on the West Indies' islands. M. P. Harris recently studied this petrel in the Galapagos, where its nesting success was extremely low, due to introduced rats and pigs. Also, as the elevated region in which it burrows is increasingly subject to farming operations, there seems little hope of it surviving. In Hawaii it is reduced to breeding, like the diablotin, on one or two inaccessible rockfaces of the interior.

The early recorded history of the world's three cool-water species of the gannet, *Sula* spp, is one of slaughter for meat. Adult gannets, like most old birds with strong muscle fibre, are tough to eat, but the flesh of young gannets, 'Soland geese', just before they leave the nest, is succulent and delicious (as I can testify, having grilled one plump fledgling which, born with malformed beak and plumage, could never have survived at sea). As a gannet is as large as a small goose it is not surprising that for many centuries the Viking peoples who settled Iceland, the Faeroes and northern and western Scotland a thousand years ago, exploited the several gannetries off those coasts.

Today only three communities, in Iceland, the Faeroes and the Outer Hebrides, still collect the young 'gugas', in late summer when they are fattest, weighing more than the adults. No adults are killed, and enough young are left to ensure future harvests. Even this annual event has become more of a traditional exercise, almost a form of sport involving boating and cliff-climbing.

The inaccessibility of many of the gannet's colonies, and its wandering sea life, undoubtedly preserved it from extinction during the world-exploration phase. But at Bird Rocks in the Gulf of St Lawrence, where the birds were heavily plundered, a government order was necessary to protect them in 1904, and in 1919 Bird Rocks was declared a sanctuary.

This was the period of a real beginning to the present world-wide movement to conserve wildlife; and the North Atlantic gannet, its numbers censused today about every ten years, has shown a steady increase. From an estimated 'low' of 50,000 birds in all colonies in 1889, the figure today is around 200,000—the greatest increases being in the gannetries of the south-western British Isles (Grassholm, Wales, from 20 pairs in 1860 to 16,000 pairs in 1972; Little Skellig, Ireland, from 30 nests in 1880 to 20,000 nests in 1972). Small new colonies have established naturally in the last two decades, on both sides of the Atlantic.

In the southern hemisphere, the Cape gannet *Sula capensis* has been heavily exploited for its eggs, flesh, feathers and guano. But the harvest is now limited, and it may soon be totally protected for the sake of its guano. There are two main colonies: about 25,000 pairs at Bird Island, Algoa Bay; and some 40,000 pairs on Malagas Island, Saldanha Bay, in the Republic of South Africa.

The third true cool-water gannet species is the Australian *Sula serrator*, with a population today fluctuating around 28,000 pairs, of which less than 1,000 nest in or near Tasmanian waters, and the rest in New Zealand. Here the Maori people were once as active in taking gannets for food as they were on their traditional forays to collect muttonbirds (shearwaters and petrels). Captain Cook, on his famous circumnavigation of New Zealand in 1769–70, discovered gannets breeding only on isolated stacks and islets difficult if not impossible to climb. Since they were first afforded protection by the New Zealand government, gannets have increased considerably and spread to more accessible islands; and there is also an increasingly large gannetry on accessible ground on the mainland at Cape Kidnappers, North Island. (This was so named by Cook because hostile Maoris there attempted to kidnap a Polynesian boy from the *Endeavour*.)

Thousands of smaller sea birds are still an important item of food, fresh or cured,

Auks such as this razorbill fly as little as possible, on short rapidly whirring wings and using their webbed feet as additional steering vanes

in all oceans of the world. Thus the traditional capture of puffins and other auks with fowling nets continues in Iceland, the Faeroes and Norway, although less than formerly. Kenyan and Arab tribes take terns and their eggs on coral islands. Shearwaters are harvested on islands off Tasmania and New Zealand, and sold as 'mutton-birds'. Thanks to international agreement to reserve the Antarctic continent and its islands as permanent sanctuaries for wildlife, sea birds breed there unmolested, though much studied, by man—a temporary visitor. But in the Arctic the resident Eskimo people of Greenland and Canada, and the Samoyede and other hunting tribes of northern Eurasia, have from time immemorial taken sea birds and their eggs for food. So long as their weapons were home-made, of wood, bone, stone and animal gut, the effect on sea-bird numbers was negligible. They were locally migratory peoples, their numbers limited by the available food supply and by the harsh winters. Today it is no longer possible for the Eskimo to subsist simply on the products of his hunting; he has become 'modernised' and money-conscious, shooting to sell, in order to buy ammunition, motor-boat or motor sledge, a house, and modern foods and clothes. Some arctic animals too are threatened, polar bear and walrus to the point of extinction.

Finn Salomonsen has summarised the recent state of the hunting Eskimo in Greenland, where the human population, exclusively attached to the seashore, has increased to about 46,000 individuals. The taking of birds and their eggs does not play as large an economic role as sealing, whaling and fox-hunting, but is still an important source of food. Salomonsen estimates that about 750,000 thick-billed guillemot or Brunnich's murre *Uria lomvia* are killed annually, equivalent to 825 tons of meat. A murre cannery has been erected in Upernavik.

The eider duck *Somateria mollissima* is probably the next most important article of sea bird food in Greenland; its eggs were also extensively taken and it has declined alarmingly in the present century from over-shooting. The Greenland government has promulgated laws, varying locally to restrict hunting, and eider down may not be collected until the nests have been abandoned in mid-July. Other migratory sea birds are taken in only limited numbers because of their inaccessibility, or other difficulty of habitat, except the little auk, a species which breeds only in high-arctic Greenland, remote from all but the Polar Eskimoes of Thule district; here so many millions of auks breed that some colonies are never visited by man, who takes them with dip-nets—many thousands annually.

The puffin *Fratercula arctica* in Greenland suffered from the collection of its eggs, which could only be accomplished by breaking open its burrows. For this, and possibly other reasons (see page 89), it has been declining rapidly. The Greenland government gave it 10 years total protection in 1961, which has at least reduced the rate of decline. Razorbill and black guillemot *Cepphus grylle*, nesting in broken-down cliffs and under boulders, are freely shot, but no decline is yet reported. The fulmar is the only petrel breeding in Greenland, and hungry Polar Eskimoes take it on its return to the cliffs in April. (I have eaten adult fulmar in Iceland, and found it tasted like the newspaper might—if one ate newspaper. The young fulmar is said to be very palatable, however, and the egg even more so.)

GUANO PRODUCERS

Exploitation of large sea-bird colonies for their guano is as old as coast-dwelling man's history as a tiller of the soil. Sea-bird faeces are richest of all natural dung in organic nitrogen and phosphate. On temperate northern shores, the lushness of the grass and the diversity of flowering plants below the ledges where fulmar, guillemot, razorbill and puffin breed are often noted. Under the cliff cities of the auks in naked arctic lands the vegetation is several times more luxuriant than upon the open tundra; but this rich deposit is unexploited as yet: marketing difficulties are insuperable, and moreover guano cannot be handled profitably in a cold wet climate: although rain encourages a lush growth of vegetation, it also rapidly leaches away the mineral richness. But on desert coasts with almost incessant sunlight, the faecal droppings dry rapidly, and have great commercial value.

So great is the demand for this natural fertilizer that artificial islands have been erected offshore on arid coasts for the roosting and nesting of local sea birds. For instance, near Walvis Bay in South-West Africa, wooden platforms about 500 x 300ft have been built on piles a quarter of a mile from the land. Here a mixed assembly of pelicans, cormorants and gannets—they are diurnal in habit—fill the platforms each night, and some remain to nest in the season. Each evening thousands of cormorants and hundreds of pelicans arrive in long skeins, each species settling upon its special roosting area on the wooden surface. The first arrivals line the edge of the gigantic wharf, and succeeding flocks of the same species drop in behind, forming uniform rows with almost military precision. Here and there a small group of gannets, and a few oyster-catchers, take up their separate quarters, apart, like uniformed officers attending a full dress parade. At last the platform is full, no more birds can squeeze a place without causing a fight to develop; any latecomers, warned off by regiments of stabbing bills, drop to rest on the sea which, on that exposed coast, forever rolls its high surf through the stoutly braced piles supporting the platform. Storms frequently damage these structures, but the guano deposited there, collected periodically and brought to land in containers slung on overhead cables, pays a handsome profit above capital and maintenance costs.

On this, the desert coast of South-West Africa, the rainfall is virtually nil. The shore is almost barren and would be completely if it were not for heavy dews and morning mist which provide enough moisture for certain drought-resistant plants to grow. Thus the rich mineral content of the deposited guano on both natural island and artificial platform is never leached away, but, dried by the hot sun and wind, accumulates in concentrated form. The longer this material is left uncollected the richer it becomes; breeding birds bring in seaweed and sticks to build their nests which, after the young are fledged, become flattened into the guano layer, adding iodine and potash to the deposit.

The annual yield of dry guano harvested from south and south-west African seabird roosts and breeding colonies has averaged 3,791 short tons in 12 years 1961-72; which is small compared with that from the South American 'nitrate coast' of Peru and Northern Chile. The monetary economy of the Peruvian government for more than a century rested largely on the yield of guano from its Bird Islands. Artefacts of Inca origin have been found in lower levels of the guano beds, indicating extraction by man at least nine centuries ago; while radio carbon $C14$ tests suggest a Pleistocene origin for the first (lowest) deposits. Incaic laws limited the extraction of guano to equal the amount of annual increment. On the penetration of the Pacific by large sailing ships early in the nineteenth century, the exploitation of the ancient deposits began. By the middle of that century large fleets of sailing ships—British and United States mostly—were carrying away about half a million tons annually, a rate of depletion of the deposits, some originally 20m thick, which gradually levelled most of them to the bare rock. The removal of the ancient beds incidentally destroyed the breeding territory of thousands of Peruvian penguins and diving petrels which had dug their nesting tunnels under the surface.

Today the guano islands are managed on a conservation basis; the harvest depends entirely on the amount of guano deposited each year. Each of the three species nesting in the open excretes about 3oz wet weight in 24 hours. Usually each island is 'scraped' clean of excreta, nests, dead birds, eggshells and feathers (all are grist to the mill which produces the saleable end-product) every other year. Since 1946 guano-producing birds have been encouraged to extend their nesting and roosting activities to certain peninsular headlands of the adjacent mainland, by the provision of fences or walls to exclude terrestrial predators. This policy of total protection has resulted in a steady increase in the tonnage extracted, from around 20,000 tons in 1900 to more than tenfold by 1971.

A new threat to the guano industry has arisen from the recent excessive netting of the anchovetas (*Engraulis* species) for the production of fish meal and fertiliser, by the large fishing fleets of Peru and other nations on the west coast of South America. But once in a cycle of seven or more years fish, fishermen and guano birds suffer a disastrous reverse when the warm equatorial counter-current (Il Nino) makes a longer annual excursion than usual south along shore, pushing the cool waters of the Humboldt Current away from the Bird Islands and the fishing grounds (see page 61). The sea temperature rises by as much as 5°C, plankton dies, the anchovetas disappear, the fishing fleets remain in harbour, fish processing factories close down, and if Il Nino persists for long enough there, the cormorants, pelicans, boobies, penguins and diving petrels die by the thousand. In succeeding good years the numbers of the guano-producers are gradually restored.

A visit to these bird islands off the coast of Peru is then an exciting experience. Some forty of them rise from the cool waters of the Humboldt Current in sight of the steep and arid mainland. As you approach, the sky darkens with millions of guanay cormorants *Phalacrocorax bougainvillii,* alcatraz pelicans *Pelecanus occidentalis*, and piqueros or Peruvian boobies *Sula variegata*. In vast skeins they ripple overhead in traffic lanes between roosting stack and feeding grounds. Each fishes in its specific fashion, making combined operations workable without severe competition. The cormorants swim in loose formation, rounding up the immense shoals of anchovetas, those in the rear flying forward to feed ahead of the submerging centre, rather as starlings feed on grassland by short leap-frogging flights. The boobies plunge perpendicularly from the sky, often in formation, as if at a given signal, disappearing in a wide curtain of spray. The pelicans make shallower dives, seldom vanishing below the surface, but scooping and shovelling fish into the landing net of the pouch. Deep below these surface-feeders, Peruvian penguins and diving petrels attack the smaller components of the food chain, along with predatory fish (bonitos, dolphins) and sea lions.

TOO MANY PEOPLE

There are other aspects, mainly deleterious, a few beneficial, of man's impact upon the numbers and survival of sea birds. His penetration of remote coasts, and his unceasing spoliation of the shore with building and holiday activities, leave less

83

space and privacy for the nesting of other than a few common land birds, such as sparrows, starlings, and some of the more sedentary gulls. On the credit side, by providing new food sources (albeit fortuitously), man has assisted some species to become more numerous. Birds are opportunists, and flock to city and parish refuse dumps where they find much edible trash—as do rats, mice, foxes, dogs and cats. Gulls especially exploit the garbage by day, and seek food at sewer outfalls. Gulls, waders, crows and other scavenging birds are also attracted to the settling tanks there by the rich invertebrate life which breaks down the sludge.

Certain species of gulls, not truly oceanic wanderers, have become largely dependent during non-breeding periods on a continuous local supply of edible wastes; and some live much on handouts of scraps at town parks, bridges and lakes. Some gulls have even begun to nest in the parks, on the banks of reservoirs, or on tall buildings. Others follow the farmer's plough and cultivator as they turn up insect and other invertebrate life. The huge increase of several species of *Larus* gulls within the present century is without doubt due to this gratuitous and varied food supply; an increase most marked in the northern hemisphere, where the more resident *Larus marinus*, *L. argentatus* and *L. ridibundus* may be ten or twenty times more numerous than they were in 1900. In North America, where the great black-backed gull *L. marinus* hardly nested before that date, there are now several thousand pairs breeding. In the southern hemisphere, the related black-backed species *L. dominicanus,* and the smaller silver gulls (*L. novaehollandiae* of Australia, and *L. scopulinus* of New Zealand), have increased in the same proportion around centres of human density.

When they return to nest on the islands and cliffs, the increased numbers of large *Larus* gulls take more eggs and kill greater numbers of adult and young of the smaller sea birds, such as puffins, guillemots and other auks, which are already declining for reasons suggested in this book (oil pollution especially). Conservationists, alarmed at the decline of the auks, have attempted control measures by sterilisation of the eggs of the big gulls, and shooting and trapping at the nest.

OCEAN SCAVENGERS

The rise of the motorised fishing industry during the twentieth century has brought a colossal output of waste protein in the form of unsaleable and small fish, and offal from stored fish, which is thrown back into the sea. Among truly oceanic birds, the main scavengers behind fishing vessels are gulls, skuas, gannets, boobies and many species of the petrel family. Most of these opportunists have at least maintained their numbers.

The most spectacular increase in the petrel family has been that of the North Atlantic fulmar *Fulmarus glacialis*. In 1947 the writer and Stephen Marchant, during twelve days of observation from a trawler fishing the Rockall Bank, 150 miles west of the Outer Hebrides, Scotland, concluded that the hitherto unexplained extension of the fulmar's breeding grounds from the Arctic south over the coasts of north-western Europe must be associated with the availability of the—in aggregate—thousands of tons of waste fish thrown overboard day and night by the vast fleets of trawlers and other vessels fishing within the 100 fathom line of those coasts. For the fulmar's spread has coincided closely with the huge development of this fishery (Figure 7). Subsequently our theory was accepted by James Fisher (1952),

(*Facing page*) Blue-footed booby pair, male on left Galapagos Islands

who added that as the spread from the Arctic began about 200 years ago, although very slowly at first, it may have been initiated by the availability of offal from the arctic whaling industry, which flourished in the century and a half before the motor-trawler boom, and which was based close to the fulmar's breeding grounds there. Finn Salomonsen suggests that if the spread of the fulmar was due to the fishing industry, a similar increase should have occurred in the western Atlantic, from colonies in northern Greenland and arctic Canada; but apparently this has not been the case, in spite of fulmars attending the large number of fishing vessels off Greenland and south to the Newfoundland Banks; therefore, he argues, the spread of the fulmar may be due principally to a genetic factor, to a genotypical change in the subspecies or strain of southern (boreal region of the eastern Atlantic) fulmars involved, in this instance evidently based on the great colony on St Kilda estimated about 1750 to be at least 40,000 breeding pairs. When a species starts to expand its range explosively (the collared dove in Europe is a recent vivid example), far into new territory, it must surely be due to an abandonment of the bird's strong instinct to return to breed at the place of hatching, and a new ability to colonise—at first in single pairs or in small groups—by mutant individuals.

Probably both theories hold good; they are not incompatible. It is true that the fulmars of the high Arctic, which have smaller bills and a larger proportion of dark-plumaged birds, appear to be static, with no new colonies; while the longer-billed St Kilda type, with less than 1 per cent of dark individuals, are the colonists. Some of these young boreal fulmars marked in western Europe reach the Newfoundland Banks during their non-breeding period.

This is the stuff of evolution: an adventurous strain of a sedentary species is born, abandons home ties in the adolescent years, and eventually colonises new ground where it has discovered an adequate food supply, in a different, warmer or cooler climate. As discussed in Chapter 1, in hundreds of years of isolation from the ancestral stock it becomes a subspecies, and at last a species. At some stage of their evolutionary history pioneer fulmars have crossed the equator (where none is ever seen today) to evolve a new species at breeding grounds around the other Pole, some 10,000 miles from the haunts of the original stock.

Two other events have undoubtedly assisted the more recent increase of the boreal strain of the fulmar in the eastern North Atlantic. At its ancestral home of St Kilda, up to the evacuation of the human inhabitants in 1930, many thousands of fulmars were killed for their flesh, oil, fat, and plumage: today St Kilda is a national nature reserve where fulmars breed unmolested. Secondly, in Iceland and the Faeroes (almost certainly colonised from St Kildan stock in the years previous to 1750 when the Westmann Islands, South Iceland, were invaded; fulmars did not settle in the Faeroes until after 1800), where many more thousands of fulmars were killed annually, about 1936 psittacosis appeared, causing sickness and death among wildfowlers; the taking of fulmars has since been forbidden by law.

However, the fulmar may be in for a less prosperous period. Many new trawlers are fitted with machinery for converting waste fish and offal into liver oil, fishmeal and fertilizer, which fetch high prices today. Significant too is the new and profitable practice of ring- or seine-netting, by which every living organism which is unable to pass through the meshes is removed from the sea, and no edible offal thrown away. When this huge net, mechanically shot and hauled in, completes the encircling movement at the surface, the footrope, several fathoms deep, is drawn together,

(*Facing page*) Part of the colony of 17,000 pairs of gannets on Grassholm, Wales

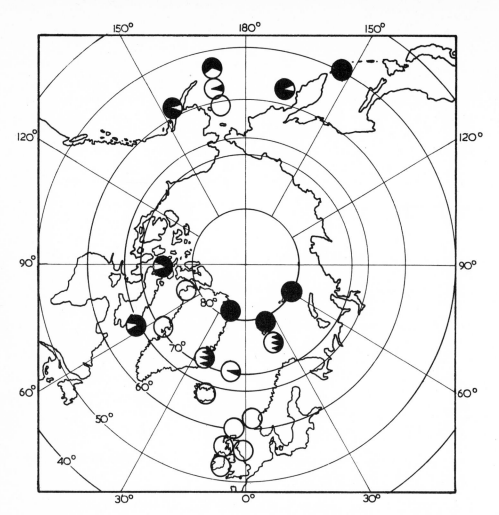

Figure 7 Breeding distribution of the northern fulmar, showing the approximate preponderance of dark birds in the populations, indicated by the dark parts of the circles (*from Fisher, 1952*)

closing all escape for the fish within. Included in the haul may be small whales, porpoises, seals, sea-lions, sharks and other large fish which, if they fail to leap over the floating headrope, are hauled aboard with the shoals of smaller fish, emptied into the hold en masse, and battened down. One haul may often be as much as two seine-boats can carry back to the factory, where the edible fish are prepared by canning or freezing, and the balance chopped up for processing as protein meal and fertilizer.

POLLUTION

Although the waters of the open ocean are wide and deep enough to dilute, absorb and neutralize most of the organic sewage (in limited quantity the nitrogenous material contributes to the nourishment and growth of swimming animals), insoluble elements, especially mercury and radioactive chemicals from inorganic discharges, persist as residues which are carried far and wide on ocean tides and currents (they have reached arctic and antarctic waters), to be absorbed in the food chain of living organisms, from plankton to the largest marine creatures. It is believed that the build-up of toxic chemicals now recorded in the bodies of, especially, the larger species near the end of the food chain, is leading to a loss of fertility, and consequently a decline in numbers able to reproduce successfully—as it has done in many land animals. (We are not too concerned with the loss of fertility in man, however!) Most of this toxic discharge enters the sea via river estuaries, carried there from factories upstream, with some pollution from artificial fertilizers applied to farmland and leached into drains and ditches. Sick and dying fish are part of this pollution. Swept downstream, they are eaten by scavenging birds and other aquatic predators, or die and disintegrate: in any case their burden of toxic chemicals is passed on—to poison the marine environment.

Another persistent, but more obvious and increasing, source of direct mortality is the result of the world exploitation of crude oil and its transport by sea. Despite new international agreement on legislation to forbid pollution of inshore waters by deliberate cleaning-out of ships' oil tanks at sea, this continues. The discharged oil floats and is driven by wind and current to the land. Other spillages are due to leakage from refineries on shore, from oil rigs offshore, and from collision or wreck. Research has shown that after the oil's volatile elements have evaporated, the sludge-like residue over many months sinks to the bottom, where it is covered with organic detritus descending from the upper layers; bacteria and other minute organisms attack and disintegrate it—as they do the tarry residue which clings to rocks above low tide, and which disappears after a few months of weathering. But the newly discharged oil slicks, floating for days and weeks at sea, cause severe mortality to birds. Particularly vulnerable are the less aerial, surface-swimming species, such as the auk family (puffin, razorbill, guillemot or murre, little auk, the several auklets), penguins, diving petrels and sea ducks. These depend entirely on their ability to dive and capture their fish and other food under water. Some, probably most,

North Atlantic fulmar, a highly successful coloniser of north-west European coasts

are flightless for a week or two during the wing moult at sea, and so are doubly at risk. Significantly there has been a considerable decline in the numbers of these swimming and diving birds frequenting the main tanker lanes. Thousands have been and are still being washed ashore, dead or dying from the effects of this filthy waste. By matting the feathers it destroys the natural insulation provided by the cushion of air, plumage and down which protects the skin from direct contact with the water; the resultant heat loss is followed by severe chill, and death from pneumonia; and the end may be hastened by poisoning through the afflicted bird swallowing tarry matter sticking to its tongue during its desperate efforts to clean its feathers.

The families of the shearwaters, petrels, gannets, gulls and terns, do not seem to have experienced such a high mortality. Although they make frequent shallow dives in feeding, it is thought that they can see, perhaps even smell—for oil slicks have a nauseating stink—the lethal discharge and so avoid the area, which in any case exhibits no live sea-food at the surface to attract them.

So far the Arctic and Antarctic oceans have been little troubled with heavy oil pollution, thanks to their remoteness from shipping lanes and their outward-flowing currents; fortunately for the flightless penguins of the Antarctic, which would be extremely vulnerable—as has been shown by the heavy mortality of the jackass penguin of the Cape of Good Hope, affected by oil pollution from tankers using the southern route from the Gulf of Arabia oilfields to the Atlantic, following the closure of the Suez Canal.

7 PENGUINS

Restricted to swimming and walking, the flightless penguins are not great wanderers of the ocean, yet some swim considerable distances, even hundreds of miles, after leaving home as fledglings; and while they are immature some remain far at sea for another year or two. Yet however far they may voyage from known breeding grounds they possess that same marvellously accurate sense of direction of the flying bird (more appropriate one should say, of the migrating whale), of awareness of their geographical position in relation to their birthplace on land or ice. In penguins accurate navigation is essential, especially in those which nest on the antarctic ice-shelf, perhaps dozens of miles from the sea.

The aquatic skill of penguins is remarkable. The wings, lacking normal flight feathers, are short and narrow, with flattened bones and muscles, and cannot be folded. Applying the aerodynamics of flight in a denser medium, the penguin literally flies under the water, beating its flippers, which almost touch on the upstroke, like those of the swimming turtle. There is high manoeuvrability under water: a sudden flip over or pivot of the wings reverses direction; the heavy feet assist only in steering. In their book *Penguins*, Sparks and Soper describe how, in pursuit of its prey, the penguin withdraws its head into its shoulders, its feet flattened against its tail, presenting a smooth lozenge shape offering least resistance to forward movement. Swimming speeds range from 5·4 to 9·6 mph. Top speed is exceeded when the penguin is pursued by its dread enemy, the leopard seal. Then, and also when in a mood of play, penguins will make porpoising leaps clear of the water, sometimes in a school. The typical bold leap from the sea, to reach a rock or ice ledge several feet above, has often been filmed.

Gentoo penguins occupy a tussock ridge with elephant seals in South Georgia

Substantial weight, heavy bones, lack of air sacs, and little air trapped between the short stiff feathers cause the penguin to swim low at the surface and to sink easily. Underwater observation and experiments at holes in the ice off Cape Crozier, Antarctica, have shown that emperor penguins can stay below for at least 18 min, and reach a depth of 265m, possibly a record for any bird. Thermo-regulation is achieved by the thick layer of subcutaneous fat (blubber) beneath the dense fur-like plumage.

The continuing researches of observers in the Antarctic today have further revealed the astonishing life-histories of the three truly polar penguins, adapted to live and breed on the ice, and to feed if need be under the ice. Largest of all penguins, the emperor *Aptenodytes forsteri*, 4ft tall and weighing up to 45kg, actually breeds on the fast ice attached to the antarctic mainland *in winter*, when temperatures fall to $-40°$C, high winds bring severe blizzards, and there is no sunlight. To offset these hazards the emperor colony, rarely less than several hundred birds, and often thousands strong, during periods of high winter gales huddles together within a compact circle. Periodically the outer individuals move into the mass for a warm-up; in calm weather the birds spread out more loosely. Thus the normal high internal body temperature is maintained, assisted by the thick layer of fat beneath the dense plumage which insulates the large plump body. Coming ashore at the beginning of winter, the emperor female lays her egg in May. The male immediately places it on top of his feet and beneath a thick fold of belly skin which protects it from frost.

The emperor colony is now halved by departure of the females, which walk the long ice road through winter darkness to the sea. They remain at sea for the whole of the incubation period of 64 days, leaving the fasting males huddled together as they keep themselves and the eggs warm. On her return from feeding at sea the female finds the ice shelf extended many miles seaward during the intense cold of the coldest months of the winter. But unerringly she marches through snow, ice and blizzard straight to the colony. She calls to her mate, and he responds (voice recognition). She gives the newborn chick its first meal. The emaciated male gets none of the food stored in his mate's stomach, but marches the many frozen miles to the sea, where he takes a long recuperative holiday and regains some of his fat. Meanwhile the female nurses the chick under her belly flap. By some process not understood, the mass of food in her stomach remains undigested for much of this period, and is doled out in suitably small doses to the growing down-covered chick, until the male at last returns to take over guard, and feeding duties—from the catch stored in his stomach. Two months after hatching the chick is left while both parents go forth to feed; for warmth and safety it huddles in a crèche with other youngsters of the colony. With the winter ice beginning to break, and the ice-shelf retreating towards the pole in November, the young birds acquire their first plumage; and in December both adults and fledglings desert the breeding site, feed freely in the summer sea, and disperse in a northerly direction. Adult emperors evidently do not travel far north beyond the Antarctic Circle, for they return to breed again in March. But on their first voyages in the open sea some immature emperors have reached warmer latitudes around 50°S, and occasionally turn up in Tierra del Fuego, Tasmania and New Zealand.

Contrast the winter breeding of the emperor, so arranged that the adults are able to breed annually, with that of the related, smaller, but otherwise similarly marked king penguin *Aptenodytes patagonica*. This handsome bird takes so long to rear its chick that the majority of adults are unable to breed in the following year; and this despite living in a slightly warmer climate on the more northerly antarctic and sub-antarctic islands. After 54 days of incubation, the chick hatches between January and March, and is overtaken by the bleak antarctic winter at the crèche stage. Huddling together for warmth, the late-born chicks grow but slowly on the infrequent if substantial meals carried to them, at long intervals of 2-3 weeks, by the parents foraging in the sea beyond the ice barrier. By the time the March-born chick is fledged it is nearly a year old, and its exhausted parents now perform their annual moult. Afterwards they breed in the third season, this time starting earlier, and if they hatch the chick in January, there may be time in the same year to complete the rearing, moult and recuperation periods, and recover condition enough to breed again in the fourth season, but two months later. And so in the fifth year they will miss breeding once more.

Less than half the size and one-fifth the weight of the emperor, the adélie *Pygosceli adeliae* is the most numerous and probably the most sociable of the antarctic penguins. It nests as far south as the emperor—in the Ross Sea. It comes ashore in parties in October; forming files, each individual one body-length from the next, the adélies trek 10 to 30 miles over the ice to reach remembered breeding grounds. These are usually fairly snow-free from exposure to winds. Here they set

about collecting small stones to make a platform, upon which one, or two, bright green eggs are laid. Incubation begins with the first egg, the male taking a first stint of 2 weeks, while the female goes back to sea. She relieves him for a short spell in mid-term, and he completes the period, hatching the chicks on the 33rd to 35th day. As the first-laid egg hatches first, the older chick gets the best share of the food, and if this is in short supply, the second chick may become weak and perish, perhaps snatched up by a skua. Adults which have bred several seasons seem more capable of raising two chicks; probably they are better foragers. The chicks are fed once daily at first; they form crèches at 3 weeks, as soon as both parents go to sea in order to find more food to meet the larger appetites. Gradually the adults feed the chicks at longer intervals, ceasing altogether when they are about three-quarters of adult weight at about 7 weeks. However this is the optimal season (February) for krill in antarctic waters, and the fledglings find plenty of food when they take to the sea, singly or in small groups, a week later.

Marking of tens of thousands of adélies shows that they may wander up to 100km from the nest site, but so far none has left antarctic waters or been found breeding far from the place of birth. A small percentage of marked birds have returned to 'inspect' the colony at 3 years of age, when very few settle down to breed. About 25 per cent of 4-year-old birds will nest, and 80-90 per cent of 5-year-olds. But only one egg is laid by these new breeders, which not infrequently take a different partner in the next season. Divorce is rare in long-established pairs, which produce two eggs.

Adélies have showed impressive homing ability. They have returned rapidly over featureless sea and ice when released 8 to 57km from the nest. Two out of five unsuccessful breeding males taken by air and released 3,800km (2,356 miles) along the coast returned to the breeding ground in 10 months, making an average speed of 13km (8 miles) per day. Allowing half of each day for resting and feeding, this would mean a steady progress of around 1km per hour, a remarkable achievement for a bird which cannot fly!

The related chinstrap *P. antarctica*, another black and white penguin, has rookeries in North Graham Land, South Shetlands and Orkneys, and small breeding groups on some other antarctic islands. It arrives later than the adélie, and lays two eggs, but the chicks grow faster; they do not form crèches but remain in the nest until they leave—as early as the adélies do. The immatures occasionally swim as far as the Falklands, possibly from South Georgia, where there is a small outpost colony. It is something of a wanderer, having been recorded some 2,000 miles west of its nearest known breeding place, and is probably circumpolar during its pelagic period.

The gentoo *P. papua* is the only penguin with conspicuous white on top of the head. It is circumpolar, breeding as well at the edge of the Antarctic Convergence, in the Falklands, Tierra del Fuego, Prince Edward, Marion, Crozet, Kerguelen and Macquarie Islands. It lays two eggs early; the young form crèches. Chinstrap and gentoo penguins have longer bills than the adélie, clearly associated with diet preferences in their rather warmer, more northern range.

Only five of the seventeen penguins are described here: the other twelve are still more sedentary, and do not justify much space in a book on ocean wanderers.

8 ALBATROSSES

Beautiful, graceful, tireless—these adjectives are often applied to describe the flight of albatrosses by those who, like Coleridge's Ancient Mariner, have watched them following a ship 'for food or play' for hours, even days, at sea. Sailors know them commonly—perhaps affectionately—as mollymawks or gooneys. They are the largest members of that vast order of expert ocean wanderers, the *Procellariiformes*, masters par excellence of the spacious air above the open sea. Without apparent effort they fly great distances from home during their long and seemingly leisurely life. They spend many more hours on the wing, at least as observed by day, than at rest on the water.

Large oceanic birds have solved the problem of mobility and endurance by becoming gliders, using wing-beating as a power source as little as possible and only when threatened with falling into the sea (stalling) at reduced speed. They may have to beat their wings more continuously when flying in a dead calm—one reason why albatrosses are rare, even on passage, in the equatorial doldrums. Beating of long narrow wings in still air would quickly exhaust a large bird; it must come down to rest, or else as described earlier, like the migrating stork or eagle it must find a thermal or pocket of rising air—frequently these ascend from a sun-heated surface of land or sea—upon which it can spiral into the sky, with little wing-flapping and much comfortable soaring. The albatross does this as expertly as the eagle; but it is normally a low-flying bird adapted to gale-ridden latitudes.

In theory head winds would be a disadvantage and exhaust the bird; but except in severe gales, the opposite is the case. Wind, light or strong, causes waves at sea which indirectly provide motive power in the turbulent uplift of air deflected from their windward surface. The wind does most of the work for the albatross, which has weight (=penetration) for fast gliding—in the largest, the wanderer, up to 27lb body weight. This bird has the greatest wing aspect ratio (up to 25) of any bird in the world. At sea it proceeds by 'dynamic soaring', with barely a flap of its flat, narrow, uncomplicated wings. It glides at gathering speed down-wind towards the surface of the waves, where the lower layers of air move more slowly because of friction; then shoots upward into the wind, losing ground speed as it rapidly gains height into faster-moving layers of air. At about 50ft the prevailing wind is at its maximum, and at this point the albatross's ground speed has almost vanished, but the bird is not yet at stalling point; if the wind is very strong it will glide forward still. But soon it must turn aside, and fall in a long glide down the wind, rapidly increasing speed for the next dynamic lift into the air.

Close to a ship's side an albatross, or gull, can glide longer, with fewer wing beats, because it is taking advantage of the cushion of air deflected upwards by wind additionally displaced by the ship's forward passage. Some birds appear to follow ships less for food than because they can 'rest' in flight for longer intervals of gliding than is possible away from the ship in the same wind. But invariably the bird, even when gliding at near-stalling point, overtakes the ship; losing the advantage of the artificial lift it falls away from or across the ship's bows in the down-wind gravitational swoop which gives it the necessary speed to make a long ellipse or figure of eight away from the ship, once more to turn and rise into the wind and seek a favourable gliding position, moving forward again close to the ship on the cushion of deflected air.

Albatrosses fly much too fast to be able to pick up food on the wing. They settle first on the water, and swim towards it. They eagerly devour meat and offal, especially waste fat from the ship's galley. Normally they live on squid and other fish taken at the surface, hooking it with the forceps of the long bill, making short dives as necessary to grab food first spotted with the head submerged. Like some large shearwaters they will eat whale dung (probably because of the squid remains this may contain).

As described in Chapter 5 oceanic birds normally survive hurricanes at sea by clever yet innate navigation; with plenty of sea room they drift to leeward until out of the cyclone's path, then make up the lost ground by a correction of course to bring them back to the traditional feeding or breeding area. The direction of sea-bird migration is genetically fixed, and evolved because of these regional cyclonic forces, not in spite of them; forces which in stormy southern latitudes cause certain species (arctic tern and albatrosses) to drift on a perfectly normal and regular migration around the whole of the antarctic land mass.

There are thirteen species of albatrosses in the world, of which the largest are the wandering *Diomedea exulans* and the royal *D. epomophora*; both have a maximum wing spread of 12ft. Most of us associate albatrosses with the stormy seas off Cape Horn and the Cape of Good Hope, from the many tales of whalers and sailors; and with good reason—the already mentioned strong and constant winds support their long narrow wings in gliding flight. In fact nine of the albatrosses inhabit the windiest latitudes between the Antarctic Circle and the Tropic of Capricorn, and most of them south of 40°S. These are the wanderer, royal, black-browed *D. melanophris*, grey-headed *D. chrysostoma*, yellow-nosed *D. chlororhynchus*, Buller's *D. bulleri*, shy or white-capped *D. cauta*, grey-backed and Chatham (these

two are usually regarded as subspecies of the shy) *D. salvini*, and the sooty *Phoebetria palpebrata* (two forms—dark and light-mantled).

Only one albatross lives close to the equator: the waved *D. irrorata*, about as large as a farmyard goose, is restricted to a single colony of approximately 12,000 pairs on Hood Island in the Galapagos. This colony was studied by Bryan Nelson who wondered why the species, now under protection, did not increase. The whole south-east Pacific is theirs to roam, away from the equatorial calm; and they travel far on the trade winds. The cool waters off the Humboldt current are a favourite feeding area, but they have also crossed the equator and been seen off Japan. The waved albatross has the long narrow wings of the fast glider, revels in wind, and is helpless without fast-moving air—a typical albatross which clearly originated in the south, followed the Humboldt Current north, and settled down at its equatorial limit.

Occasionally an albatross breeding in the far south has crossed the equator and lived for a while, even several years, among sea birds in cool northern latitudes, as did a black-browed albatross which remained attached to a gannetry in the Faeroes for 34 years: this species has wandered to Spitzbergen, to waters much the same temperature and containing similar food as in its southern range. But evidently not enough individuals have been able to get together in the North Atlantic to open a new colony.

Three other albatrosses however, have evidently come from the south, and now breed, as quite distinct species, in the north Pacific. Of these the short-tailed *D. albatrus* is the world's rarest albatross. Formerly breeding on small islands in the north-west of that ocean, it was much persecuted by fishermen and feather-hunters, and is now reduced to one colony of possibly 200 effective breeding adults on the small volcanic islet of Toroshima, Japanese territory, fortunately now declared a sanctuary for them. The other two are also given protection on their breeding atolls of Midway and Laysan, north-west of the Hawaiian group; these are the black-footed *D. nigripes* and the Laysan *D. immutabilis*, slaughtered for their plumage and flesh a century ago.

The two largest albatrosses, the wanderer and royal, have a closely similar life history. Obviously there has been a comparatively recent separation into two species from a common source, and almost certainly from the more numerous, more widely distributed wanderer. The adults are much the same size and colour, both white with black trailing edges to the very long wings, and are virtually indistinguishable at sea in mature plumage. Each has a larger subspecies breeding farther south, and measuring up to 50in long, bill to tail; the smaller northern subspecies may measure as little as 30in in length. But at all stages of plumage the young royal is paler in colour than the young wanderer, which leaves the nest with uniform brown upper-parts, and is several years attaining the white back of the adult. The wanderer is circumpolar in breeding range, nesting on sub-antarctic islands south of New Zealand and in the south Indian and Atlantic oceans; but the royal is confined to the Chatham, Campbell and Auckland Islands, and one headland near Dunedin in South Island, all within New Zealand territory.

The magnificent wandering albatross has been closely studied, especially at South Georgia, where probably 5,000 pairs nest. L. Tickell estimated the world population of wanderers as between 50,000 and 60,000 birds, representing approximately 20,000 breeding pairs. K. Westerskov estimated a world breeding population

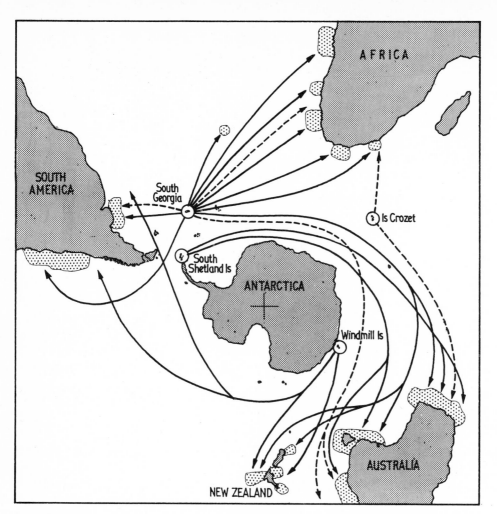

Figure 8 Probable circumpolar, wind-assisted, movement of wandering albatross (dotted line) and giant petrel (continuous line) as indicated by banding results. Circles indicate banding stations. Shaded areas are main recovery sites

for the royal of 10,124 pairs by a somewhat different method of calculation. These are rough estimates but at least they give us some idea of the numerical strength of these splendid birds. As with most large wild-bird species today they are far from abundant, although at the moment safe from extinction so long as they are allowed to breed in peace on their remote islands.

The oceanic wanderings of both great albatrosses are interesting. Because of their similarity when adult, some of the early visual records of both species within 30° and 50° in all southern oceans were considered doubtful. However extensive leg-banding has since defined their range more certainly, from recoveries of marked individuals. Wanderers from nests on South Georgia, Kerguelen and Crozet Islands have been captured off the south-east coast of Australia; a long flight for the South Georgia birds of around half the antarctic continent; and some have been recovered off the coasts of South Africa and South America (Figure 8).

Some two dozen royals banded at New Zealand sites have also been recovered far from home, on the coasts of Chile and Argentina south of 30°S, but so far not off South Africa. A few have been recaptured nearer home in New Zealand and Australian waters. There was an exceptionally heavy wreck of at least 187 albatrosses on the southern coast of New Zealand's North Island following the tropical cyclone of 9/10 April 1968, with gusts of 100 mph; 110 of these were royals (only 19 of the southern race), 26 wanderers, 45 white-capped, 5 black-browed and 1 Buller's. April is a time of moult for these albatrosses, and this helps to explain the unprecedented mortality. Most banding recoveries have been of adults, probably because few are marked as nestlings during their main (winter) growth period, when observers are generally absent from their inhospitable storm-swept breeding grounds.

The two great albatrosses take so long to rear their single chick that the pair are not in a condition to breed in the following summer. The adult male arrives first, early in the southern spring. He remains at or near the chosen site, often the downtrodden nest of a previous season; and both species choose open ground (which is convenient for their elaborate courtship manoeuvres; they do not nest on sheer cliffs), and preferably a windy site, which assists landing and take-off and does not accumulate snowdrifts which might bury the nest. The importance of the male arriving first and taking possession of a nest site is evident when the female appears for the first time: for she seldom makes more than two or three visits before the egg is laid. As a rule she alights at this early stage only for the purpose of coition, and if the mate of her last breeding season is not present, she may mate with another male—not that an experienced female deliberately seeks a fresh mate at once, but other males, alone at their nest-sites, will run out and attempt to mount a passing female, evidently able to recognise her sex from that distance. Males take no notice of other males; but on arrival of the female there is a mutual greeting ceremony of bill-clapping and wing display, which breaks down the barrier of their long separation since the last mating two years earlier—if they are mature partners; this adjustment or recognition procedure may take longer if they are young birds mating for the first time.

The nest is begun in a desultory fashion by the male, waiting alone on his chosen territory; but is vigorously improved by the female accepting material (tussock grass, moss and mud) from him in the few days before the egg appears. Quite a cup is built up, useful against bad weather in the months to come. Three to five weeks may elapse between the arrival of the male and egg-laying. Several unmated males may approach and display before a newly arrived female, but once the egg is laid the ceremonies become a simpler affair, a ritual recognition procedure by which the pair bond is strengthened. The mated pair then go through the ceremony alone, fencing with their bills, groaning harshly, opening their wings, bowing, the female rotating to face her mate as he side-steps around her. To the human observer she appears to show affection without allowing him to copulate more than occasionally; and not at all after the egg is laid. Unsatisfied sexual desire in the male seems to be channelled into a strong possessive instinct to brood the egg, and he has been observed to push her forcibly from the nest.

Usually the female remains only a few hours after the egg is laid, before the male takes over the first shift of incubation; but if he happens to be absent on the day of laying she will remain incubating (in two recorded cases up to 18 days) until he returns. The average shift is less than a week, so that the change-over occurs nine or ten times during the 78/9 days of incubation, and the male normally broods rather longer in total than the female.

The downy chick hatches from the pure white egg as winter sets in. It is brooded by the adults in turn, changing guard on average every other day, the parent at sea gathering food for it meantime. Meals are small at first, consisting of a soupy predigested liquid which is doled out as required into the nestling's mouth, its bill crosswise within that of the parent, as in all tube-nosed birds. The albatross chick will squirt vile-smelling stomach oil at an intruder at this stage, like some other petrels. On this diet the chick grows rapidly; at 32 days it weighs about 3kg, and is too large to be covered by the adult. Despite the increasing cold and reduced sunlight the parents cease to brood, and visit it for short periods only to feed it, and no longer every day. However the meals are progressively larger as they diminish in frequency. The weight of the chick fluctuates accordingly.

Sitting on its hummock nest throughout the bitter winter of these latitudes, buffeted by high winds, hail and snow, the solitary nestling wanderer or royal maintains an adequate internal temperature under the thick coat of fat it has acquired beneath its dense coat of down and sprouting plumage. The adults seem to have no difficulty in finding sufficient food on their winter visits home, which occur at the rate of approximately 3·5 feeds in 10 days. The average period during which the young bird remains in, or near, the nest must be a record for any bird: 236 days for the royal, 278 days for the wanderer chick. The last feed is usually delivered a few days before the departure of the fully feathered young albatross to sea.

This fasting for several days in the latter part of the fledging period, between large meals which produce fat reserves, is a preparation for a future when, especially during severe storms at sea, it may not be possible for the albatross to feed for several days; and when, as we have seen, it will fast for several days as an incubating adult. To a greater or lesser extent such fasting is common to all members of the petrel order, as described in succeeding chapters. Weights of 19 wanderer chicks, during 20 days in the nest preceding departure, showed a decline of around 2kg as a result of fasting or reduction in the number of feeds brought by the parent. But loss of weight at this stage, when the fledgling is strengthening its wing-muscles by regular flapping exercises, is of course a valuable preliminary to successful flight. Overfat young albatrosses find difficulty in taking off.

In most of the tubinares (fulmars, shearwaters and storm petrels) the adults abandon the fledgling, proceeding to sea on their annual moulting migration several days before it leaves the nest. But apparently this is not so in the large albatrosses: wanderer, royal, laysan and black-footed adults have been seen visiting the nest up to the day the fledgling departed, although it has only rarely been seen to be fed on its last day ashore.

The wanderer spends well over a year completing its breeding cycle, and the royal rather less:

Period in days	Wanderer	Royal	Smaller albatrosses (average)
Nest preparation	30	30	25
Incubation	79	78	64
Chick in nest	278	236	171
Total (averages)	387	344	260

At the breeding grounds of the wanderer in October and November, it is possible to see some fledglings on their battered pedestals at the same time that adults are incubating a fresh white egg on a newly built nest. Occasionally a hungry fledgling, perhaps still with down adhering will approach and importune an incubating adult for food—but in vain. This does not happen at royal colonies,

(*Facing page*) Arctic tern the world's longest distance migrant

which narrowly complete the reproductive cycle within the year, so that the breeding ground is deserted before the alternate batch of breeding royals arrives— after their sabbatical year at sea. In both species those adults which have successfully reared a chick do not breed again in the next season. Only if the egg has been lost before hatching, or fails to hatch, is there time for the owners to leave home, moult at sea, and be ready to breed in the next summer.

Having successfully launched into air and sea, all young albatrosses remain ocean wanderers for at least two years, and probably several years longer. During this period of independence they nevertheless retain visual memories of the place where they were born: visual memory (learning) is all-important to reinforce genetically coded memory (instinct). From a study of more than 25,000 recaptures of Laysan albatrosses at Midway Atoll, Fisher and Fisher suggest that visual memory of the exit pathway to the beach, established by the fledgling on its first trip seaward, guides the bird to make its first landing at the same spot on its return as a prospecting juvenile in succeeding years; each successive return reinforces the stimulus to remember and use the same pathway, and so it becomes fixed (traditional) by the bird's first breeding season years later.

Some young wanderers begin to return to prospect their future breeding grounds 3 years after they have fledged, that is at 4 years of age; royals apparently are a year or two later. But although they may land and indulge in courtship, even nest-making, the activity of these adolescents is tentative, somewhat perfunctory, and too late in the season for egg-production. Not until it is at least 6 years old does the young wanderer establish itself as a breeder, by adopting territory and a mate at a site which has gradually become familiar during those preliminary visits. Even so the female may not lay her first egg that year. L. E. Richdale considers that the female royal does not normally produce her first egg until she is 9 years old.

So the two giant albatrosses, breeding only once (successfully) in 2 years, and reaching 6-9 years before starting to nest, must be long-lived. To maintain their present numbers each pair must rear to maturity two replacements, which will take them a minimum of 4 years. But we must allow for normal mortality, which has been assessed as follows:

% mortality at stages:	Egg/chick	1st Year	Adult (annual)
Wanderer (Tickell, 1968)	41	61	4·3
Royal (Westerskov, 1963)	25	10	10

These figures are divergent. But Westerskov calculates that of the 19,000 royals of the southern race on Campbell Island, 47 per cent are breeders, the balance of 53 per cent being non-breeders up to 8 years old. In Tickell's theoretical calculations for wanderers quoted above (a world population of 50-60,000 birds of all ages), one-third would be adult breeders; and he suggests that, although fewer birds survive the earlier years of immaturity, a larger proportion of adults live to old age. This, for a giant albatross, is probably in a few instances up to 80 years or so.

How far adult albatrosses range for food while breeding is not known, but certainly several hundred miles would be no obstacle. Long absences during the incubation period may be associated with recuperative feeding after fasting; for their breeding grounds are all within a few hours' flight of the upwelling zones rich in squid, crustaceans and fish.

(Facing page, above) Female grey phalarope in breeding finery, Iceland; (below) Red-necked phalaropes in breeding dress, Norway

Like other petrels, albatrosses will attend whalers and fishermen, as well as picking up edible garbage in the wake of ships. They can be caught on hooks baited with meat or fish, and were once a source of protein to Polynesian people who took them on lines with fish and bone hooks, from their canoes offshore—or even, when glutted with squid and other prey, and too sluggish to rise from a calm surface, with spear, net or noose. A thrown hoop-net and noose have been used to capture, band and release, from small boats, hundreds of large albatrosses in Australian waters (see Figure 8). This banding at sea has traced the wandering of some of the great albatrosses during their alternate free year as adults without family cares, and, as already remarked, some birds drift and glide west to east around the world south of latitude 30°S, before the strong westerlies of the roaring forties.

It has also helped to show that the nine southern-hemisphere albatrosses share their oceanic ranges in an interesting pattern; although not yet fully deciphered, this suggests that each has a different ecological (food and distribution) niche. All but one begin nesting in the months of the southern spring or early summer, even the three North Pacific species—again suggesting a southern origin for the latter. The exception is the waved albatross of the Galapagos, which lays its eggs in April or May, but there is of course perpetual summer on these equatorial islands.

All the *Diomedea* are colonial breeders; in contrast the *Phoebetria* (sooty) albatross is a lone nester on steep cliffs and precipices where the young bird seldom has room to wander safely from the nest; like the kittiwake gull in the same situation it must start its flying life with the first glide into space. The sooty is the most graceful of all albatrosses, its exceptionally long wings and tail giving it the utmost flexibility in aerial manoeuvring.

The life-history of the smaller albatrosses follows much the same pattern as described above for the two giants. The lesser species have shorter breeding seasons, and 3 months 'resting' period in the year; but may not necessarily breed annually. While the waved albatross normally feeds in the trade-wind zone of the Humboldt Current south of the equator, it is interesting that the flight range of the three North Pacific albatrosses is well to the north of the calms of the equator, and extends from their breeding grounds in the Hawaiian chain and Japan north through wind-troubled seas to the Aleutians. Feeding in the same latitudes north, as their cousins do in the south, these gooneys come home to nest in the breezy northern winter, in the same months as their relatives are breeding in the southern-hemisphere summer. Probably the prototype albatross which first made the crossing to settle north of the equator was an ancestor of the present blackfoot, which shows more primitive features than the other northern gooneys, and a closer affinity with the southern albatrosses.

Blackfoot and Laysan gooneys co-exist on some islands and atolls, the dark-plumaged blackfoot—a clumsy walker—breeding on bare open sites, the elegant white-breasted Laysan, preferring some cover of rough ground or scrub. Probably they speciated as a result of the blackfoot, soon after colonising bare atolls in the north, overflowing to other islands with scrub cover, and developing into the present refined-looking Laysan gooney. Finally the considerable shortage of suitable islands in the albatross zone of the North Pacific brought the new Laysan back to nest on the same atolls as the blackfoot. Although hybrids occasionally, but rarely, occur, apparently they are not fertile: the two gooneys have become genetically isolated as true species. Greeting and dancing ceremonies are vulgarly

Black - browed albatross showing the typical feeding procedure by regurgitation common to all petrels

boisterous in the blackfoot, more restrained in the Laysan, and there are other behavioural differences which, with the differences in colour, make it difficult to break down the barrier of individual distance. In any case the typically long period of association in albatrosses between members of a new pair before copulation occurs does provide time and opportunity for 'second thoughts'—or, in more scientific terms, for correction of interspecific alliances (Fisher, 1972).

The albatrosses have little fear of man or mammalian predators, which rarely invade their remote breeding islands. I have sat beside and stroked the head of an incubating royal albatross, after making a slow crawling approach—violent movement close to the nest will release their defence reaction of opened wings and lunging bill. The tameness of gooneys and their determination to retain their nesting sites when Pan-American Airways built runways for their transpacific clippers on Midway Atoll in 1935 was embarrassing. As air traffic increased the number of bird-plane collisions multiplied in ratio of about 1 albatross killed or wounded to 2·5 planes operating; and 1 in 15 of these encounters resulted in serious damage to the plane. To clear the gooneys from the runways area various powerful noise, smoke and odour deterrents were tried without success. The gooneys slept on their nests undeterred, or continued to glide down the tarmac and build new homes at will. Nor did they budge when a golf-course was laid out for the use of visitors to the new hotel (appropriately named Gooneyville Lodge; the golf-course was billed as unique in the world for having albatrosses nesting in the fairways). Bombing raids by the Japanese air force in the Pacific war had little effect. They survived the elimination of thousands of nests and sitting birds by the defenders in repeated efforts to reduce the 'gooney-hazard' to aircraft. Destroying the gooneys nesting alongside the airstrip actually had the effect of increasing the numbers of albatrosses landing there, as non-nesters flew in, attracted to any depopulated space, in a flourishing gooney colony, as a possible future breeding site. At the end of the war there were still 110,000 Laysan and 53,000 blackfoots on the 1,600 acres of Midway, a total only slightly less than their present capacity numbers.

At last investigating ornithologists seconded from the US Wildlife Service noticed that the gooneys were using the currents of air deflected upwards from natural dunes and artificial buildings near the runways, just as they use those deflected from waves for their dynamic soaring described earlier. By levelling these, and by widening the tarmac, this uplift zone was reduced in area, and collisions became rarer.

Apart from man, albatrosses seem to have few enemies. Egg and chick losses from avian predators, and the man-introduced brown rat, are slight. But C. B. Kepler (1967) reported an alarming predation by the small kiore or Polynesian rat *Rattus exulans*; this is distributed throughout the Pacific islands occupied or visited by the Polynesian people (and formerly eaten by them, so it was probably deliberately introduced to some islands—eg New Zealand). Out of a population of about 5,000 gooneys on the remote Kure atoll in the Hawaiian Leeward Isles, about 1,000 pairs breed. Kepler counted 50 adults dying or dead from kiore predation, and many others were probably concealed in the dense scaevola scrub. In one season deaths from rat predation brought the net loss to above 50 per cent of mature albatrosses, an insupportable mortality if continued; and albatross chicks and other sea birds were attacked. Kepler also recorded that Bonin petrels *Pterodroma hypoleuca* lay up to 500 eggs on Kure each season, but as yet no chick has been found. Excavation of petrel burrows revealed fragments of their eggs. Rats have also been observed carrying sooty tern eggs away from a disturbed colony; chicks of noddy terns were attacked from the rear, and the body cavity opened; in a two-week period the number of noddy chicks dropped from 528 to 381, a loss of 27·9 per cent. R. R. Fleet (1972) found that the red-tailed tropic bird, breeding on Kure in the northern spring, was likewise severely depleted by the kiore taking eggs and eating young alive.

Contrast this with the behaviour of this same rat on White Island off the north-east coast of New Zealand, where it is abundant in the coastal pohutukawa (*metrosideros*) forest. While in camp there with a NZ Wildlife Service party in 1965, making a gannet survey, we were regularly visited at meal times by kiore rats tamely scavenging below our table. They were numerous around the several gannetries where they ate fish scraps spilled or regurgitated by adults bringing food to the nestlings. No rat predation of the gannets was observed, or of the numerous young grey-faced petrels *Pterodroma macroptera*, near flying stage, in burrows which were undoubtedly also used for cover by the kiore.

GIANT PETREL

Equal in size to the smaller albatrosses—the heavy-looking male can be 2½ft (760mm) long, beak to tail—the giant petrel (or fulmar) *Macronectes giganteus*, with its thick ponderous bill, is frequently mistaken for a young or dark albatross. Its wings are proportionately shorter, the flight somewhat stiffer yet with much skilled gliding.

In the albatrosses the nasal openings are small inconspicuous tubes at the sides of the upper mandible, close to the face. In the giant petrel the nostrils extend as a long tube on top of the bill. The significance of these differences is not clear, but, as described in Chapter 2, the nose in the petrels is a complicated organ having several functions. In the albatrosses and fulmars, and probably in others of the family expert in fast gliding and dynamic soaring, the middle paired nasal chambers each have two valve-like pockets, the function of which may be that of an anemometer. Like the human ear drum, the valves may well be sensitive to air pressures, and serve to inform these high-speed gliders of the varying velocity of the air stream forced through the nostrils during each phase of their dynamic soaring.

From its voracious scavenging—it devours any kind of animal offal, dead or wounded birds, seal and whale carcasses, penguins, cormorants, small petrels, and their eggs or young—and its habit of squirting vile-smelling stomach oil when alarmed, together with its sinister appearance with dull rusty-brown plumage, and pale cold eyes, the giant petrel has earned opprobrious names from sailors, whalers and fishermen: stinker, stinkpot, glutton, nelly, black molly. It is the vulture of antarctic seas. On land it walks agilely, compared with the shuffling gait of albatross, fulmar and other large petrels; evidently an adaptation to nesting on flat or gently sloping surfaces, often some distance inland, and of feeding on what it can seize thereon.

From its circumpolar breeding sites, the giant petrel ranges all southern oceans north to 30°S latitude, with many recoveries of individuals (banded chiefly at Macquarie, South Georgia and South Orkneys Islands) off New Zealand, the southern coasts of Australia, South America (chiefly west coast), and South Africa (Figure 8). It ranges the Humboldt Current north to Peru, but is rare close to the equator. One of the largest colonies is in mid-South Atlantic, on the Tristan da Cunha Islands.

Born with a whitish down, a few giant petrels acquire white plumage when adult; a colour phase relatively more numerous close to the antarctic coast. A mottled white form occurs in lower latitudes, as at Macquarie Island.

The spring courtship of the stinker petrel has been described by Racovitz, who noted that the males raised and spread their tails 'as if they aspired to be peacocks, and danced before the seemingly unresponsive females of their choice'. The fact that they were hideously smeared with blood and grease from seal carcasses upon which they had been feeding did not in the least dampen their amorous behaviour.

At the nest the adults are devoted partners, and tenderly care for the single egg and chick, sharing the shifts of incubation and brooding, as in other petrels. When closely approached by a human visitor both adult and chick behave like the fulmar petrel, squirting the stinking stomach oil from the open mouth pointed at the intruder, and, if the internal supply is generous, not without success in hitting the target. However some giant petrels go through the motions without bringing anything much to the surface, and adults that have been a long time on the nest may be quite dry. After 100 days in the nest the fledgling is very fat, and abandoned by its parents; and goes to sea alone during the next fortnight, after a fast.

Tales of giant petrels attacking human beings, other than drowned floating bodies, are highly exaggerated. After vomiting towards you, the adult shows timidity if the approach is pressed home, and abandons the nest. This is the opportunity for the bold sheathbill and the nimble skua to dart in and snatch the egg or baby chick before the petrel dares to return. These are its few natural enemies; although neighbouring giant petrels, if sufficiently hungry, have been known to devour eggs and chicks, and the wounded or dead of their own species. The fearsome hooked bill is a lethal weapon for tearing apart its normal prey, and it has been seen to kill a rat with one swift blow.

9 FULMARS, SHEARWATERS AND OTHER PETRELS

The other, smaller members of the vast family of tube-nosed birds share the food resources of all oceans in a fascinating if complicated interlocking ecological pattern, each group with distinctive feeding habits and regions.

The fulmars are scavengers; the shearwaters live on live fishes, squid and crustaceans taken near the surface; the storm petrels feed at the lowest levels of the marine food chain, skimming the minute crustacea and larval forms floating at or near the surface; the prions (whale birds) sift and strain their food through specially adapted beaks as they scoop the planktonic bloom from the top layers of cool southern waters; and diving petrels behave like the northern auks, chasing their small prey below the surface. But their life-histories are built on much the same pattern as that described for the albatrosses.

After leaving home the young bird wanders at sea for one or more years within a prescribed area before it returns to settle, after several visits, at or near its birthplace. Once they have bred, male and female normally remain faithful to the site and so to each other so long as both shall live. At each meeting on land, after the lengthy excursions at sea, there is a greeting ceremony. Recognition is by voice rather than sight.

Young petrels, from giant albatross to least storm petrel, become extremely fat just before they are fledged. Their stomachs bulge with oil-saturated food after each visit by a parent. At this stage, heavier than the adult, they are (or were) eagerly collected by local hunters, who extract the oil, and eat the tender flesh. So oily are young petrels that when collecting them the hunter will hang them up by the bill to prevent the oil trickling out of the mouth until he is ready to squeeze it into a container. Predators which eat young petrels at this stage may become thoroughly discomfited by oil-saturation of their plumage or fur. Young sea eagles, released on Fair Isle in 1968 in an attempt to re-establish them in Scotland, so gorged themselves on the abundant fledgling fulmars there—which doubtless vomited upon them before being torn apart—that their feathers became matted with oil, reducing their capacity to fly in the autumnal gales so that they were swept to death by drowning in the sea. (Experienced adult eagles must know how to cope with this danger: fulmars are a favourite food of cliff-dwelling eagles in the northern hemisphere.)

Millions of 'mutton-birds', Tasmanian shearwaters, were eaten by the white colonists of New South Wales, fresh, salted or in pies. The fat was used to grease friction surfaces in the early saw-mills and coal mines. Today mutton-birding is restricted to the collection of fledgling short-tailed shearwaters *Puffinus tenuirostris* by less than 200 licensed Tasmanian residents. In 1968 nearly half a million mutton-birds were sold, worth per 100 $14 salted, $16 fresh. The oil from these is used pharmaceutically and in sun-tan lotions; the fat mainly as a supplement to enrich skimmed milk fed to farm stock.

All petrels are more or less gregarious at the breeding grounds, even though individual nests on cliffs and burrows may be far apart. Fulmars and a few of the larger shearwaters nest in the open, but all the smaller shearwaters and petrels lay their single white egg in burrows dug in the ground or in crevices deep in talus and boulder accumulations, or under dense vegetation. Thus they are protected from their many predators above ground, and from exposure to harsh weather and, in a few tropical species, to excessive heat from the sun. These burrow-nesters are almost all nocturnal in visiting and leaving the burrow, from the same innate fear of diurnal predators; although these habits do not protect them from nocturnal enemies such as rats and owls, or from the occasional flooding of burrows during a cloudburst.

A few tubinares fly far inland to nest in holes on high mountain ridges and cliffs, in bare screes or under rain-forest vegetation, for reasons we have already suggested. Examples include: the diablotin of the forested mountains of Hispaniola; the Hutton's shearwater of the naked Kaikouras at over 4,000ft in New Zealand, where at the same or lower elevations elsewhere several large dark petrels nest in bush-covered scarps; Hornby's petrel breeds in the desert of the high Andes; Manx shearwaters inhabit the mountain crags of Rhum Island, in the Hebrides, and above 5,000ft on the Madeira sierra; and several medium-sized petrels nest high up on the tree-clad volcanic peaks of Pacific islands. Fulmars will nest far inland on ice-free cliffs and nunataks in both Arctic and Antarctic lands.

FULMARS

Fulmars are the 'mollies' of the northern latitude sailor. They are graceful in flight, and their dark-ringed eye in the white face enhances their beauty. In southern waters the southern form *Fulmarus glacialoides* is sometimes called Cape dove, from its pale appearance compared with its darker speckled relative, the Cape pigeon. Some sailors regard the mollies with awe and perhaps a little affection; the super-

Fulmar

stition, also attached to the albatross and storm petrel, lingers that each molly is the reincarnation of a person drowned at sea.

James Fisher in his monograph on the fulmar agrees with K. H. Voous that during the Pleistocene glacial periods when the polar ice had pushed breeding sea birds towards the equator, the antarctic fulmar must have colonised the North Pacific first, where it subspeciated from the parent stock. Then in a warmer period this offshoot, now dubbed *F. glacialis rodgersii*, penetrated the Atlantic via the Arctic Ocean and, breeding much farther north than in the Pacific, developed into a dimorphic form of *glacialis*, the dark phase predominating in the high arctic breeding grounds of northern Greenland, Baffin Island and Spitzbergen, where the population appears to be static, and has smaller bills. Taxonomists argue as to the validity of the subspecies some have made of *glacialis*, separating the dark northern form as *F. g. minor* on these morphological differences and because it seems to live in ecological and geographic isolation, having a separate breeding and winter range. *Minor* apparently seldom leaves high or low arctic waters.

The typical Atlantic *glacialis*, with only a small minority of dark-phase individuals, with its centre of breeding probably at St Kilda, ranges the boreal coasts of western Europe; and ringed individuals have wandered far north-west into the range of the high arctic birds during their non-breeding period.

As already mentioned the popular theory that polar-breeding animals, including birds, tend to be paler (if not pure white) to match the snow and ice, than their relatives breeding in temperate latitudes, does not work for the fulmar. The Pacific fulmar exhibits a larger proportion of dark birds in the southern part of its range; at the northern breeding colonies (St Matthew and Pribilov Islands) in the Bering Sea, only 20 per cent are dark. As there are also intermediate colour forms, and bill and body measurements overlap, it is safer at present to lump the northern fulmar races under one specific name, *glacialis*, given by Linnaeus. And the southern (also known as the antarctic or silver-grey) fulmar, which is a pale bird with rather longer wings and a longer more slender bill, breeding entirely south of the Antarctic Circle but wandering farther north into sub-tropical waters than the northern fulmar flies south, remains *glacialoides*; first named by A. Smith in 1840.

Both species have almost identical life-histories. The southern fulmar is a bird of the ice in summer, nesting on antarctic cliffs, especially on islands. All fulmars are almost helpless on land, walking with difficulty, and so they fly direct to the narrow nesting ledge. Here, territorial and courtship rituals take place, resembling those of the albatrosses—they consist of mouth-opening and cackling and head-nodding, but there is no room for wing display. The single egg is incubated by both parents, in fairly long shifts, and hatches in about 55 days. The young bird remains on the ledge for an average of 46 days, being deserted by its parents about a week before departure, during which there are the usual wing-flapping exercises and reduction of excessive fat.

CAPE PIGEON AND OTHER ANTARCTIC PETRELS

Probably the best known and one of the most numerous of the wandering birds of the southern oceans is the Cape pigeon *Daption capensis*. Easily recognised by its magpie appearance, mottled black and white in flight (speckled haglet is one nickname), it can be observed far from its breeding grounds in Antarctica and the sub-antarctic islands. It follows the Humboldt Current to Peru, and rarely across the equator. In cool southern seas it appears behind ships as if by magic when meat or fish offal is thrown overboard. For its size, that of a large pigeon, it is scarcely less voracious than the giant petrel, attacking weak and wounded birds, tearing at carcases of whales and seals. Normally however, it feeds on euphausian and other plankton-eating small fry. Harrison Matthews describes how the wide upper bill,

Cape pigeon

with its fine serrations overlapping when the beak is closed, and the throat pouch, are used in feeding in much the same way as described for the prions (below). Minute particles are hooked up by the tip of the bill 'with a few drops of water, in rapid succession into the mouth, and the pouch is quickly expanded and contracted so that the water is strained off at the sides of the bill and the food particles retained on the serrations. When feeding in this manner the bird keeps vigorously paddling to each side with its feet, so that it only moves forward slowly and a current of water is drawn in towards it from the front.'

Noisy and quarrelsome when feeding at sea, it is a poor shuffler on land, and never ventures ashore to feed. For the same reason, like the fulmar, it nests exclusively on steep cliffs, pitching directly upon and launching itself from the nest site. This is commonly lined with rock chips and other material pulled in from around the spot. The single egg is incubated and the chick reared in the usual fashion of tubinares, through guard duties by both parents.

It is surprising that the Cape pigeon has not established itself in the northern cold-water oceans, since it is so ubiquitous and abundant in the southern. It is a very distinct genus, with no near relations; perhaps the prions are closest.

Two other related petrels nest in the same inhospitable antarctic environment with the Cape pigeon, and although they rarely leave the vicinity of the pack ice and icebergs, deserve mention here for their remarkable adaptation to the south-polar climate. The snow petrel *Pagodroma nivea* is as white as its name implies, save for a dark-rimmed eye, black bill and dark grey feet—giving it a beautiful dove-like appearance, which is also a protection: the bird seems to vanish when it settles on the ice and snow of its environment. It breeds on the antarctic continent, often far inland, selecting high crags. One colony has been found on the granite cliffs and screes of King Edward VII Land, more than 80km from the sea.

The antarctic petrel *Thalassoica antarctica*, a brownish bird 17in long, with white belly and patches on the wings and rump, nests in the same polar situations. Thousands may inhabit holes and niches in the steep slopes of mainland and island cliffs and mountains. They are often seen feeding between ice floes on the abundant euphausian shrimps, or at rest upon the ice.

WHALE-BIRDS OR PRIONS

Although not great wanderers, the prions or whale-birds *Pachyptila* are remarkable for their sifting method of feeding, as described above for the Cape pigeon. R. C. Murphy in *Oceanic Birds of South America* writes that whale-birds 'offer beautiful examples of the phenomena of differential growth, which is alone sufficient to account for what I regard as four species of the single genus'. And he illustrates the point with the sketch (Figure 9) of bill sizes and shapes. Other taxonomists have made eight species on the evidence of bill size, plumage pattern and distribution.

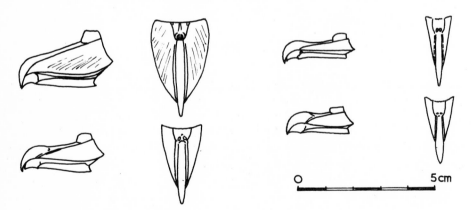

Figure 9 Lateral and superior aspects of the bills of four species of whale-birds; all represent males. Top left pair: *Pachyptila vittata*, bottom left: *P desolata*, top right pair: *P belcheri*, bottom right: *P turtur (after Murphy, 1936)*

The evolution of these partially migratory birds is still in the melting pot. Isolated in their local regions, their genetical variations tend to stray in separate directions. All are adapted to feed on the teeming small crustaceans—the feed of the baleen whales of the same latitudes; hence the vernacular names of whale-bird, scooper, ice-bird. The largest, the broad billed *P. vittata* has the greatest development of ridges or lamellae along the inner edge of the bill, a sieve-like arrangement, against which the large fleshy tongue works in expelling water from and retaining food in the large distensible throat pouch.

Enormous numbers of the antarctic whale-bird or dove prion *P. desolata* were recorded by the explorers Weddell (1825) and Ross (1847) in the seas now named after them. Millions of these little petrels (less than 300mm long) formerly bred in the stony screes of South Georgia, but, as on other islands, introduced rats have reduced their numbers. The normal long incubation and rearing period of this species, which does not lay its egg before the snows uncover its burrow in November in the Antarctic, means that the fledgling is often trapped by the first winter snow; but usually it is able to tunnel a way out.

After a blizzard it flies with astonishing accuracy to alight on the snow-covered site of its burrow at night. Tickell, who studied the dove prion in the South Orkney Islands, tested its homing ability, and found that marked individuals could return over 500 miles in 50 hours and over 770 miles in 5 days. He concludes that a feeding range of about 100 miles from home during the breeding season is probable.

All prions, because of their powerful diurnal predators, especially skuas, gulls and giant petrels, arrive at and leave their holes in the darkest hours of night. In the northern limit of their range some colonies have been exterminated by cats on certain islands; and only on the smaller rat- and cat-free islands have they survived in good numbers. Both the largest *P. vittata*, and the smallest (fairy prion) *P. turtur*, may nest on the same islands, as they do on the Snares and Chathams of New Zealand, yet, with quite distinct bills and body size, they do not hybridise, or seem to compete seriously for territory or food.

Seventy years ago the Scott Polar Expedition ornithologist and artist E. A. Wilson described the tireless twisting fast flight of prions. They remind me of the manoeuvres of starling and wader flocks, as, densely packed, they wheel above the water, white breasts flashing at one moment, then at the next their dark upperparts cause them to vanish against the background of the sea. Normally they feed as they swim at the surface, scooping up and straining their food; but I have seen them making short shallow dives.

SHEARWATERS

Like the prions, but on a world-wide scale of distribution, the shearwaters display an evolutionary pattern of differential size, structure and plumage, closely related species sharing but not competing for the oceanic food resources and breeding sites. Man has attempted to classify these into subspecies or races on their often slight differences of size, colour and habits, as well as their breeding distribution. All species of shearwaters have virtually identical reproductive habits: long incubation and fledging periods, shared parental duties on the shift system, and desertion of the large fat nestling some days before it is fit to take to the sea. The large shearwaters, with their powerful flight, share the same or a similar food spectrum in all oceans of the world (a few penetrate in summer the Arctic Ocean), in a pattern which is meaningful to the observer, for it suggests the economical use of the available but limited suitable breeding territory, and full exploitation of wintering grounds by long-distance migration, as discussed earlier.

A further adaptation to territorial pressures seems to be the use of the same burrows by related species breeding at different seasons. The winter-nesting grey

Cory's shearwater

shearwater or pediunker *Procellaria cinerea* occupies burrows and crevices on the Tristan da Cunha Islands vacated by 2–3 million summer-breeding great shearwater or hagdon *Puffinus gravis*; the hagdon flies north on its long tour of the North Atlantic during the austral winter (the northern summer), returning when the pediunker flies south to enjoy the southern summer, wandering and moulting in circumpolar seas (Figure 10).

Another large shearwater *Puffinus diomedea*, not easily distinguishable at sea from the great, and formerly known as the North Atlantic great (but now Cory's) shearwater, makes a migration exactly opposite to that of the Tristan great shearwater: breeding on temperate islands in the North Atlantic and Mediterranean in summer, it 'winters' in the southern summer off Brazil and South-West Africa. I have studied this powerful bird on the eastern Atlantic islands of Berlangas (Portugal), Desertas (Madeira), and Salvages (north of the Canaries), where it is known as *cagarra*, and *pardela*, from its hoarse screaming call. Here it is the dominant petrel, but too large to enter the small burrows occupied by three smaller petrels: the little shearwater *Puffinus assimilis*, the frigate petrel *Pelagodroma marina*, and the Madeira or Harcourt's petrel *Oceanodroma castro*. On the Salvages I found the three smaller petrels occupying the same burrows, but varying their dates of egg-laying so that each possessed the burrows for a reproductive period of 4 months, so covering the 12 months of the year without serious overlapping. How this nice sharing of the burrow accommodation came about is not clear; but competition probably forced the weaker or later-arriving of the three, driven out by the species in possession, to postpone its nesting to the period it now uses for successful breeding. As already discussed, some petrels of the same species nest at different times at different sites, even though the climate and latitude are more or less the same. And some tropical petrels seem to have no fixed breeding season. David Snow found that in the Galapagos the Madeiran petrel has an egg-laying season once every 6 months.

In the Pacific and Indian oceans the large flesh-footed *Puffinus carneipes* is the representative of the Atlantic great shearwaters, and like *P. diomedea* has been divided into subspecies (even species) on slight differences in colour and distribution. As

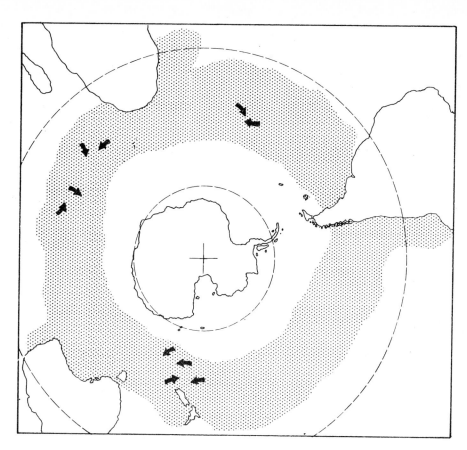

Figure 10 Distribution of grey shearwater *Procellaria cinerea*. Breeding sites arrowed, marine range shaded

shown in Figure 11, the eastern form *creatopus*, paler and usually white below, breeds on islands off Chile. The all-brown western form breeding on New Zealand islands, migrates clockwise north to Japan and to coasts off North America, where it mingles with Chilean-born relatives. The Australian *carneipes*, on the other hand, migrates across the Indian Ocean to tropical waters north of Madagascar.

Studying the flesh-footed shearwater on Eclipse Island, south-west Australia, John Warham found that it gathered in large rafts near the island before sunset and awaited nightfall before coming ashore. It is a summer breeder. Its large burrows are barely vacated before the winter breeding grey-faced or great winged petrel *Pterodroma macroptera* begins spring-cleaning. Egg-laying dates are nicely separated by 6 months. Here too the winter-breeding little shearwater *Puffinus assimilis* occupies the smaller burrows, and so does not compete territorially with the large shearwaters.

The newcomer to bird-watching in the Pacific has some difficulty in the accurate field identification of several other shearwaters of similar size, shape and colour. For instance Buller's shearwater *Puffinus bulleri* and the wedge-tailed shearwater *P. pacificus* both have wedge-shaped tails, and are the same size, and although Buller's is much paler than the southern forms of the wedge-tailed, the latter has a light phase breeding both in the north Pacific and Australia.

Slightly smaller, the dark-brown mutton-bird or sooty shearwater *P. griseus* makes a long transequatorial migration from its temperate southern ocean nesting

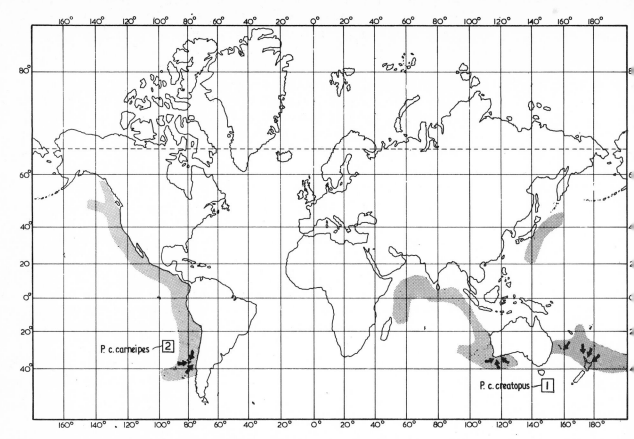

Figure 11 Breeding site and range of flesh-footed shearwater, *Puffinus carneipes* two subspecies: 1 *P.c. carneipes,* 2 *P.c. creatopus*

grounds to reach waters of the same temperature in the northern hemisphere summer. On their first return to the breeding grounds the adolescent sooties do not land, or only briefly; instead they wander further south to within sight of the antarctic ice at times, during the austral summer when the adults are busy nesting. It is rare in the Indian Ocean but common in the north Atlantic where it associates with great shearwaters *P. gravis* making their clockwise northern migration during the austral winter. It is abundant then in the chilly waters of the Sea of Okhotsk, and common in the Bering Sea, where it mingles with another dusky brown southern 'mutton-bird', the Australian slender-billed or short-tailed shearwater *Puffinus tenuirostris*, on its offseason cruise (Figure 12).

Thanks to the extensive banding studies of these two 'mutton-bird' shearwaters on the Bass Strait islands, we now have a true picture of their annual cycle, extraordinary migration, longevity and other facts of their life-history. These parallel those made in the even longer study of the Manx shearwater *P. puffinus*, a task I had the good fortune to begin over 40 years ago, and which has been continued ever since by other observers, on Skokholm Island, Wales; over 100,000 have been banded there. These studies have shown that, like the albatrosses, these shearwaters do not breed until their fifth year or later. After mating at the burrow the female goes off to sea to feed heavily for several days while the egg is ripening in the oviduct. The single white egg is laid on a remarkably constant date in the spring, and the male takes the first shift of incubation while she takes another rest period at sea. Medium shearwaters hatch their egg about the 53rd day; and the chick remains on land between 72 days (Manx shearwater) and 90 days (mutton-birds).

On its clockwise migration of hardly less than 20,000 miles around the Pacific, the slender-billed mutton-bird penetrates farther north than the sooty; and, passing through Bering Strait, it is common under the midnight sun along the edge of the floating ice of the Arctic Ocean (Figure 13). Breeding success in all three shearwaters is such that, under protection on certain islands where they are no longer collected for food, they have increased almost to the capacity of the islands to provide adequate nesting holes. A few marked individuals have lived 20 years under observation, which must be near the limit for a small sea bird.

It is now considered that there are eight races of the Manx shearwater. The very clear black-and-white nominate race breeding chiefly on west coasts of the British Isles, with small colonies in the Faeroes and Westmann Islands (Iceland), has been shown, by the extensive banding already mentioned, to migrate south to Brazil and the Argentine coasts in the autumn. The adults return early in the new year, and spend much time in February and March feeding in the sardine-nursery area of the inner bight of the Bay of Biscay. They may even fly to this favourite feeding zone during off duty spells, while the other partner is incubating the egg, a journey of 600 miles, or 1,200 both ways. Later, as the young sardines migrate north in early summer, the shearwater's forays will be shorter; the large adult sardines spawn in the English Channel in the late summer, when they are known as pilchards,

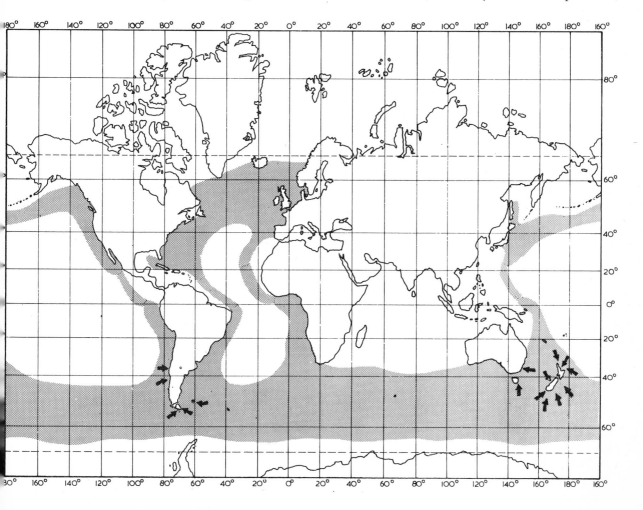

Figure 12 Sooty shearwater, *Puffinus griseus*. Breeding sites arrowed, marine range shaded

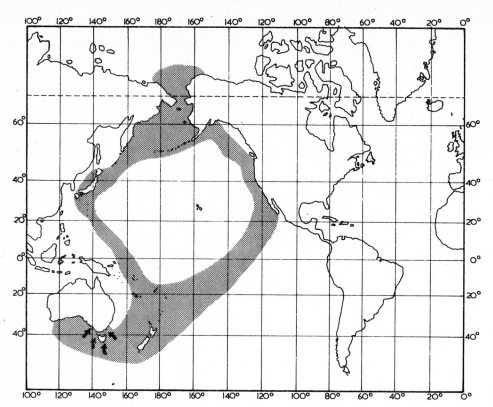

Figure 13 Short-tailed shear water, *Puffinus tenuirostris*
Breeding sites arrowed
marine range shaded

but the immature sardines return south to Biscay during their first autumn, pursued by the southward-migrating shearwater flocks.

Banding also shows that this race of Manx shearwater, during its first two years at sea, makes a more leisurely north-eastwards passage in the northern spring than the fully adult, which hurries back to claim its breeding burrow. Leaving Brazilian shores on a clockwise migration, assisted by tradewinds, the nonbreeder flies past Bermuda and towards Newfoundland and the rich fishing banks, where it may linger until August in its first year, and may return to winter quarters without touching the European coast.

Figure 14 shows the distribution of the subspecies in Atlantic, Mediterranean and Pacific waters. Little is known about the movements of the other subspecies, since only the Manx has been extensively banded; but the Mediterranean *maureticanus*, a browner bird, regularly migrates north to the south coast of the British Isles (after sardines?) and even to the North Sea. In general the variations in plumage have led taxonomists to divide the species into races, following a recognisable pattern of black above and white below in those which breed in the cooler northern or southern waters, and of brown above and dusky or offwhite below in those breeding nearer the equator. The New Zealand fluttering shearwater *gavia* is no great traveller, however, and remains more or less in home waters all the year, crossing the Tasman Sea as far as eastern Australia. Until 1965 the breeding grounds of the closely allied Hutton's *P. huttoni* were unknown, although it was commonly seen around the South Island of New Zealand, and as far west as the whole south coast of Australia. As mentioned earlier, it is slightly larger and has a longer, more slender bill than the fluttering, which it otherwise exactly resembles, but is two months later in commencing to breed—at above 4,000ft in the Seaward Kaikoura

Figure 14 (*Facing page*
Breeding distribution of the
Manx shearwater — super
species—*Puffinus puffinus*

Figure 15 Breeding dis
tribution of the species-pair
the little shearwater *Puffinus
assimilis*, and Audubon'
shearwater, *P l'herminieri*

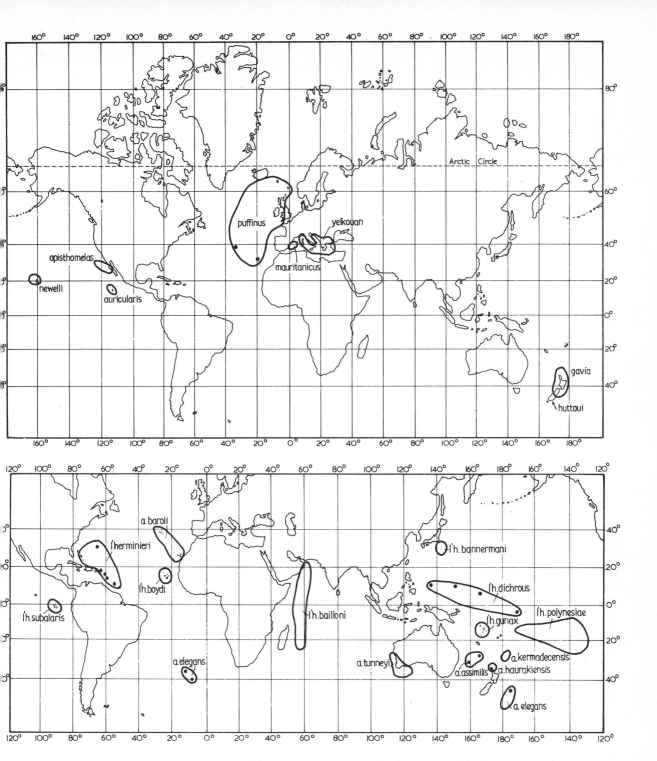

Mountains of the South Island. These differences between the mountain breeding *huttoni* and *gavia* nesting on small islands are clear enough to warrant some taxonomists giving them specific rank. The longer wing of *huttoni* suggests that it is a greater traveller.

There are no such clear differences in bill or colour in the colonies of highly migratory Manx shearwaters breeding on small islands and sea cliffs in north western Europe and those which breed in the screes of high mountains (Madeira and the Hebrides); they are identical, and probably maintain this homogeneity through a small but frequent exchange of young colonists.

Smallest of the *Puffinus* genus, the little or allied shearwater *P. assimilis* is typically resident in waters near its breeding grounds, which has assisted it to subspeciate in isolation into recognisably distinct races. A winter nester, it often occupies burrows used in summer by more powerful petrel species. As Figure 15 indicates, it is a cool-water breeder, and in the tropical zones is replaced by the Audubon's shearwater *P. l'herminieri*, which, only locally migratory, has likewise subspeciated considerably, in all three oceans. These two 'least' shearwaters are a species pair, also conforming to the general rule of the shearwaters, of dark or black and white belly plumage in cool waters, and dusky or browner upper surface in warmer seas.

GADFLY PETRELS

The *Pterodroma* or gadfly petrels also pose a problem of identification at sea. There are numerous species and subspecies, and they come in several sizes varying from 11-18in (280-460mm) in length. Too little banding has been carried out to be sure

Gadfly petrel

of the extent of their migrations; but in general they disperse rather than travel long distances. The mottled petrel of New Zealand *P. inexpectata* is an exception: it has frequently been seen as far south as the edge of the pack ice in summer; and evidently some travel north to winter in the cool water off Alaska (several records). The gadfly petrels breed as far south as Kerguelen, but most species are found in warmer seas, and of these the story of the rare cahow *P. cahow*, the diablotin *P. hasitata*, and the Galapagos *P. phaeopygia* has been told in Chapter 6.

STORM PETRELS

Although the smallest of the great tribe of tube-nosed birds, the fragile-looking storm petrels inhabit all oceans between Antarctica and Iceland and the Aleutians.

Storm petrel

Some are wanderers, the majority comparatively local in their range. Most notable wanderer is Wilson's petrel *Oceanites oceanicus*, which breeds farthest south of all storm petrels. Millions of these dainty birds, not much larger than a sparrow, frequent the pack ice in summer, easily identified by their long legs with yellow centres to the webs with which they skip and walk over the surface, in butterfly-like flight. In the austral winter they fly north to concentrate in dense numbers in areas of high plankton-counts, such as the Newfoundland Banks, the Humboldt Current, the Gulf of Aden; and even the Red Sea is visited. Figure 16 shows this distribution, and the breeding sites of the two forms. The large antarctic subspecies returns to the snow-covered land during November. Any crevice into which it can squeeze may serve as a nesting site, and there is much competition for holes in frost-shattered screes. B. B. Roberts found it in Graham Land burrowing into deposits of peat under patches of moss. The same burrows are used year after year although some may contain frozen eggs or chicks in various stages which died in the previous season. Most of these casualties are due to heavy snow blocking the entrances; the adult is able to unblock the entrance if the snow is freshly fallen and not consolidated.

Roberts noted that the Wilson's petrel pair sit side by side, alternately preening each other, with some bill fencing, as I have watched the storm petrel at home on Skokholm. In the Welsh climate there is little need for a cosy nest, and the storm petrel often incubates on the bare soil; nor does Wilson's petrel, rather surprisingly, do much more than add feathers and dead moss to produce a cup-shaped lining, hardly adequate to insulate the egg from the zero antarctic summer temperature. As observed in some other burrow-nesting sea birds, such as shearwaters and puffins, nest-making is haphazard and continues in a desultory fashion throughout incubation, and is more of a displacement activity by one or other of the pair during temporary frustration of the sexual or brooding drive. It is essential therefore that once the egg is laid, one or other parent keeps it warm for the 43 days of incubation; and here the strength of the desire to brood results in a change-over every 48 hours. The Wilson's petrel chick is born late in January or early February, and—again typical of the shearwater and petrel family—it is some 24 hours or so after breaking a breathing hole before the chick struggles out of the egg. It remains weak and helpless for a similar period, during which it is carefully brooded, and fed on predigested oily food.

Born with a soft straggling down, the storm-petrel chick acquires homiothermic

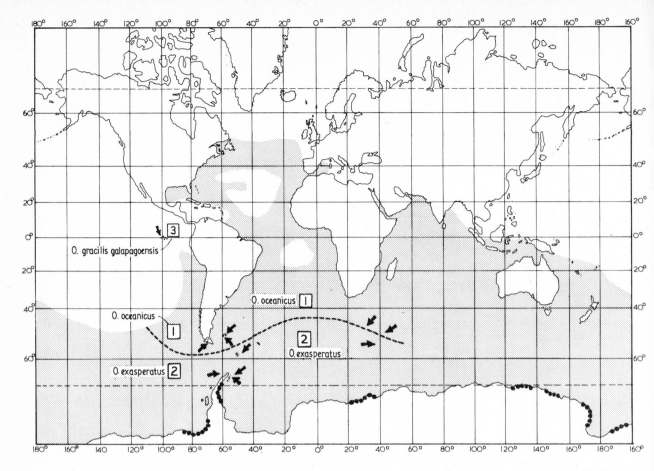

Figure 16 Wilson's petrel *Oceanites* species. Breeding sites arrowed, marine range shaded

resistance to cold within about a week, having put on fat rapidly; and is then left alone by day while the parents gather food. If they fail to return to the nest because of heavy snow or other reasons, the chick can survive for several days, gradually becoming more torpid as its temperature drops. In Wilson's petrel this ability to conserve energy during an enforced fast may save the chick during the long rearing period of 2 months which ends with the onset of the first winter snows. Roberts found that the parents would clear away up to 20cm thickness of new snow in their efforts to reach and feed the entombed chick at this stage. About the sixtieth day of its life the young petrel is normally fatter and heavier than the adult, and is then abandoned. It fasts for several days while remaining in the nest, hardening its new flight feathers; and at last makes its first flight to the sea, alone and usually by night.

R. C. Murphy at South Georgia, and other observers in the Antarctic, have noted the surprising fact that Wilson's petrel is immune to the attacks of the skua, which is such a dread predator of larger petrels, penguins, cormorants, and endemic ducks.

The smaller subspecies of *oceanites*, breeding on islands off southern South America (Cape Horn, the Falklands) makes a shorter winter migration, apparently keeping to the cool water of the Humboldt Current without crossing the equator. At the equator itself the representative *oceanites* is *gracilis*, a race found only in the Galapagos group, where it is resident, seldom wandering far from the land.

Leach's petrel *Oceanodroma leucorrhoa*, much the same size as Wilson's, appears to fill the same breeding niche in the northern oceans as the latter does in the southern. It has been divided into at least five races (Figure 17). It is less of a wanderer, and does not enter the Indian Ocean. Leach's is long-winged, with buoyant erratic flight, rarely pattering on the water as it dips and dives for its minute fish and crustacean food. It does not breed until at least three years old, and is very gregarious, with concentrations of burrows in selected areas of the small islands where it nests.

The name 'petrel' is said to derive from the habit of walking on the water—after St Peter. And there was formerly a common superstition that the 'stormy petrel' (any petrel in fact) is a sacred bird because each one is the reincarnation of a person drowned at sea, as already mentioned. They are 'Mother Carey's Chickens', gathered in a flock commanded by that legendary, benevolent, if sinister female deity of the sea: sinister because these tiny birds appeared close to a ship in distress in a gale, ready, so sailors thought, to carry off the souls of persons soon to be drowned. Formerly a sceptic in the matter, I at least understood how the legend arose when, during a voyage from the Rockall fishing grounds in a small trawler, I watched the true storm petrel *Hydrobates pelagicus* feeding confidently close in the wake of the ship as she rolled and laboured heavily, running before a gale of Force 10, her propeller churning up planktonic food. With their white rump and fluttering easy flight they resembled feeding house-martins: dainty webbed feet pattered on the broken surface as they steered with marvellously skilful control of flight. By hugging the water closely they gained protection from the worst effects of the gale which was making the trawler heel to leeward.

As discussed in Chapter 2 all the petrels have a powerful musky smell, which is particularly noticeable at the nesting site, from frequent ejections of the stomach oil. At Skokholm it was possible to locate the nesting sites of storm petrels during the

Figure 17 Leach's petrel, *Oceanodroma leucorrhoa* races, distribution and breeding sites

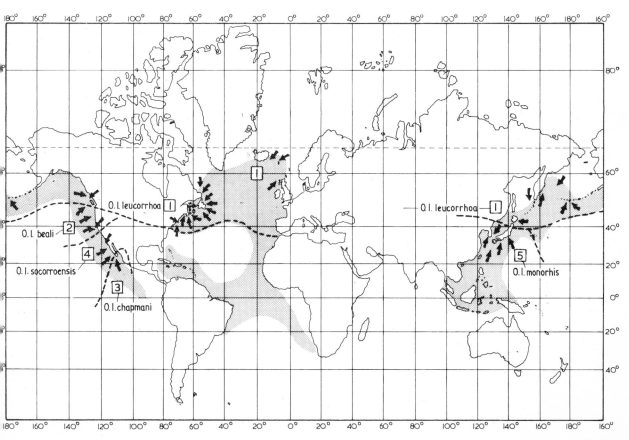

day, when no petrels were visible, by 'sniffing' in likely places (the old stone-lined hedge-walls were fruitful) with your nose close to the crevices. But it is certain that between petrels at night recognition is by voice only: the storm petrel has a pleasant purring or crooning song. This is the signal familiar to its mate during the pre-egg courtship stage, the intimacies of which takes place in the darkness of the nest-hole. The incoming bird behaves like the homing bee; in the twilight of the oceanic night I have watched the mated storm petrel circle in a tightening spiral over the nesting area for a few seconds before alighting precisely at the entrance to its burrow.

From their breeding quarters in islands in the eastern North Atlantic and the Mediterranean, some storm petrels fly far south to winter in the summer seas off South Africa, the smallest sea bird to make such a long journey.

DIVING PETRELS

As already mentioned, the diving petrels *Pelecanoides*, known to sailors simply as 'divers', are unique in structure and habits among the tube-nosed birds, and,

Diving petrel

although true petrels, they occupy in the southern hemisphere the biological niche of the auks of the northern hemisphere. They are stocky short-winged birds about as large as a large storm petrel. Like the auks they obtain their food entirely by diving, using the wings to paddle or fly through the water. On land they are nocturnal in visiting their burrows. In the air they are laboured, whirring along as straight as a bee. For a while they are flightless, during the annual moult at sea. There are five or six species, confined to the stormy latitudes between 35°S and 55°S; except one species *P. garnotii*, which has wandered north in the cold Humboldt Current to become endemic, and more or less sedentary along the arid coasts of Peru and northern Chile. The Peruvian species digs a burrow in the guano deposits of the Bird Islands. Living in a calmer hotter climate, and enjoying a bounteous supply of food in the cool water along this coast, it breeds at any time of the year; it has contradicted Bergmann's law which lays down that the nearer the subspecies or species is to the Pole, the larger it must be to resist heat loss. The Peruvian diving petrel is a good deal larger than the most southern form, the antarctic *P. georgicus*.

10 TROPIC AND FRIGATE BIRDS, GANNETS AND BOOBIES

Three species of the beautiful white-plumaged tropic birds inhabit all warm oceans. When not breeding, they wander hundreds of miles from home on feeding expeditions in tropical zones where winds are light or absent. They are one of the few birds to be seen in the Doldrums, and in the middle of the Sargasso Sea's perpetual anti-cyclone. They have been placed with the Pelicaniformes because of their basic structure, but their habits and appearance are distinct. Like the petrels, their young are born covered with silky down—the other species of the order, pelicans, cormorants, gannets, boobies and frigate birds, are born naked. Characteristically, a lone tropic bird will suddenly appear out of the empty ocean, fly tamely round as if inspecting the ship, perhaps alight for a while on the masthead, make its whistling call, then leave. The long tail feathers, which have earned it the name 'marlinspike' from sailors, seem to have some sexual significance in aerial display: I have seen one bird flying above the other depress its tail so that the streamers caressed the upper parts of the bird flying below.

Phaeton aethurus, the red-billed, is the largest species, and more heavily barred with black on the back. The white-tailed *P. lepturus*, and the red-tailed *P. rubricauda*, are a few inches smaller. The two central tail-streamers double the length of a tropic bird, to about a metre.

All three live by diving for fish and squid, remaining below for a few seconds, rather longer than gannet and booby. They search for food in direct flight, with a rapid wing beat. As a rule they appear singly at sea unless there is a dense fish-shoal attracting numbers of sea birds. Even in the nesting season the tropic bird is non-social—except during the early courtship display, when more than two birds may be seen circling in aerial pursuits.

The breeding season varies according to latitude, and there is some irregularity, as in some petrels and boobies, which can be associated with the fluctuating and often limited food supply in calm warm seas. The red-billed on Ascension lays its egg in any month, with a peak of laying in August. The white-tailed (or yellow-billed), nesting on the same island, has its main laying peaks in March and December, thus not clashing with its larger more powerful cousin. The red-tailed in Hawaii has a peak of laying in March, but in the Kermadecs the southern form *roseotincta* usually lays between mid-December and mid-January.

The single egg is laid in a hole, usually in an inaccessible cliff, or some rock crevice difficult for terrestrial enemies to reach, but the red-tailed will lay under a bush on the Hawaiian atolls; and always at some distance from the next pair. The white-tailed sometimes lays its egg in a firm crotch of a tree several feet from the ground. No nesting material is gathered.

The mature tropic bird pairs for life, faithful each season to the one nest site. To this it flies direct: its small feet are unadapted for walking, and it can only shuffle forward with breast touching the ground. Incubation is shared, and lasts six weeks. The downy chick, fed by regurgitation, is brooded for the first 7-10 days. The adults go forth to fish before dawn, and on return may fly restlessly near the nest crevice for several minutes as if reluctant to land—possibly because the adult has not finished predigesting the flying fish or other bony fish food sufficiently to service the chick (the parent guillemot withholds fish in a like manner—see Chapter 12). At this stage the nestling is sometimes attacked and eaten by rats, if these are present on the island.

The fledging period is long, the nestling becoming exceedingly fat; at 40 days it is fully feathered and weighs more than an adult. At this stage it exercises its wings vigorously, but depending on how well it has been fed does not leave home until it is between 65 and 100 days old. Apparently, like the young shearwater and petrel, it is deserted by its parents, and finally flops rather than flies down to the sea. Until it has lost some of its baby fat, or until strong winds assist it to become airborne, it may swim for several days, always making haste to get as far from land as possible. Like its parents, having deserted the breeding cliffs, it will remain pelagic and mostly out of sight of land during its non-breeding life. But one day, perhaps more than a year later, the sexual drive will impel it to return home, guided by both visual and instinctive memory, to look for territory and a mate.

FRIGATE BIRDS

The magnificent frigate bird is considered to be another pelican, but its primitive bone structure is nearer to that of the tropic birds than the true pelicans and gannets. Its life story is very different, however: a sea bird wholly adapted to living aerially, never alighting on water except by accident. Its small legs are useless except for perching; it neither walks nor swims voluntarily (its plumage is said to be non-waterproof); the toes are not fully webbed; it must fly direct from a resting position by a vertical take off, or leap into space.

Of the five species the largest, *Fregatta minor* (by a curious chance the specific

Great frigate bird

name of the greater frigate remains *minor* because it was first described as *Pelecanus minor* in the eighteenth century), has an 8ft wing span, yet weighs much less than a bird such as a booby with half that span. High aspect ratio and low wing loading, enable the frigate to fly with perfect mastery of the air. Its broad curving wings and long forked tail assist in hovering in the comparatively calm regions it inhabits. Its flight differs altogether from that of another aerial expert, the albatross, which is adapted to windy latitudes. The frigate can outmanoeuvre almost any other bird: it can hover, soar, twist and glide, all with apparent ease.

Well-named 'man-o'-war' from its piratical habit of pursuing other sea birds, the frigate is essentially a resident of tropical seas, and although it has been seen 1,000 miles from the nearest land, normally it lives attached to and often in sight of a base for nesting and, since it does not swim, for roosting at night. After a whole day on the wing during the non-breeding half of the year, the frigate sleeps soundly, so profoundly that it can be captured as it snores on its perch on cliff, tree or bush!

Often gregarious, the frigates appear very beautiful and graceful as they hover in a group above a ship, gliding with ease. Their keen eyes detect the dip and dive of another bird which is fishing successfully, and instantly one or more frigates are in pursuit: they may attack an unsuccessful fisher, but if so they quickly recognise their mistake, and will concentrate on a laden bird. It is believed that the distress cry of a pursued bird varies according to the amount of food carried in its throat or crop—muffled if full, loud and clear if empty. If a loaded bird refuses to disgorge, the nearest frigate will close in and seize its tail, wing or leg and this invariably results in the contents of the crop being vomited. As the victim bends its head and opens its bill the frigate swoops beneath, and swallows the vomit in mid-air. Columbus was first to describe this behaviour, in the log of his voyage to discover America.

Boobies and terns, in particular, are severely harassed at their breeding islands by frigates which build their single nests conveniently near those of their bene-factors, whose eggs and chicks they also devour. In human terms the frigates are vicious baby-snatchers and cannibals, for they will if hungry, swoop on the un-tended nests of other frigates, and gulp down egg or young chick in mid-air. Another trick is a swift, accurate snatch to intercept food in the second it is being passed from the bill of an adult to a nestling booby. Colonies of boobies and terns, where frigates are present, often have low rearing success.

Nevertheless, away from the opportunities to attack other birds, the frigate can earn an 'honest' living. It would in fact starve if it had to rely entirely on food forced from other bird's crops. It is fast enough to catch flying fish in mid-air, and will scoop up from the surface any small fish, squid etc, its long hooked bill hardly immersed.

Although perfection in the air, the frigate bird in its nesting affairs on land seems to be so thoroughly unsuccessful that it is surprising that it maintains its numbers. To offset heavy egg and chick losses it must be long-lived—once it has achieved complete independence, a state which it takes longer to reach than other marine birds. Bryan Nelson describes the extraordinary sequence of the reproductive period at the Galapagos, confirming earlier observations by Stonehouse at Ascension, and other observers in the Bahamas:

> Successful pairs cannot breed annually or less than annually as other members of the [pelican] order apparently do. This was an unexpected discovery, which we interpreted to mean that the food situation enforces slow growth on the young, and that after fledging a frigate needs many months to acquire the tricks of its aerial trade; until practically a year after hatching it first needed feeding, and later subsidising, by its parents.

Even so, Nelson found that many juveniles began to starve when their parents stopped feeding them. Much depends on the availability of good shoals of fish to feed both the frigates and those species which they rob.

The dramatis personae in the frigate colony at the start of the season therefore include hungry juveniles from the previous season which, although they can fly perfectly, hang round supplicating for food. Their parents meanwhile have abandoned the site, and even ceased to roost near it. (Non-breeders will sleep heavily at a roost away from the breeding place.) But other adults have returned to breed, having enjoyed a rest period of several months, or else having had no success in their last season are ready to try again.

Departing from the rules of territorial behaviour common to nearly every other sea bird, the male frigate ready to breed often sits amicably with other males, generally on the tops of trees or bushes at or close to the nest site, displaying to the females which fly close overhead when they are ready to mate. Each male inflates his bare throat patch until the naked skin is blown up into a scarlet balloon which seems to force the head backwards, tipping the bill skywards, while the wings are spread to maintain balance in this grotesque attitude—'creative licence gone mad', to quote Nelson. The pumping of air to fill the sac takes several minutes and the male appears intoxicated with his efforts, no doubt further stimulated by the displays of other males hard by (their spread wings perhaps touching his), and by the presence of the plain piebald females, which lack the inflatable pouch.

On spotting a female close overhead the male pumps his balloon to the limit, pointing it at the lady, and at the same time flashing the silvery underside of his open wings as a further signal. If a susceptible female approaches, the assembled males vie with each other in an effort to win her, so that the vegetation seems to blossom suddenly with gigantic quivering scarlet flowers. But until the lady has made her choice by settling beside one, the males show no hostility towards each other. Then the unattached males rise up together, to take up a new display site; while the fortunate suitor deflates his sac, and the couple begin the serious business of nest-making.

As a rule the female waits on guard at the site for her mate to bring the few sticks which will make the crude lattice platform, resembling a dove's nest, on which she will lay her single egg. He must collect this material entirely on the wing, so his choice is restricted to breaking off twigs from bushes in flight, picking up loose stuff on the ground with his hooked bill, and—a favourite ploy—robbing the nests of neighbours, chiefly other frigates and boobies. Any bird carrying home a twig is automatically pursued by nest-building frigates. Frigate v frigate in aerial manoeuvre will provide a marvellous display of dexterity: the owner, or winner, of the twig may baffle pursuers by suddenly descending to his nest in a tight spiral, arriving home with a scream of triumph beside his wife.

The pair become model parents, although they never feed each other. For several days before she lays the egg the female guards the nest from stick robbers. When the egg at last appears, the male immediately incubates it, while she, hungry, flies away on a feeding expedition lasting at least a week. During 55 days of incubation each in turn takes stints of about 9 days. Perhaps it is as well that nest relief is infrequent since the change-over display involves dangers to the egg in flapping of large wings during vertical arrival and take-off at the flimsy, wobbling nest platform. More than half the eggs or newly hatched chicks in a frigate colony are accidentally knocked off and lost in such manoeuvres. But undoubtedly the primary reason for the long stints of alternate feeding and fasting is the uncertainty of obtaining food in a shorter period, either by piracy or by honest aerial fishing.

If short of food the frigate will even steal the egg or chick of its own or other species from beneath the breast of a brooding neighbour. It regularly snatches these from the nests of the wideawake terns of Ascension; so much so that, with added predation by cats, no young terns are reared in some seasons.

The female frigate will lay another egg if the first is lost early enough in the incubation period, and there is a fresh courtship display by the male, who temporarily reinflates his red balloon.

The chick is excessively ugly, naked, with topheavy head and heavy drooping lead-coloured bill. The heat, and stench of rotten fish, in the colony are almost unbearable to the human visitor. The baby frigate would be scorched to death in the sun if one or other parent did not continuously shade it during the first 14 to 21 days, and until it has grown a thick white down. Later, when the chick can withstand heat better, and both parents are away foraging for food, the half-grown nestling suffers further hazards from buffeting by the long wings of courting neighbours: despite brave attempts to stab at them, the youngster may be toppled from its platform.

Nelson remarks that the male will display anew each year and accept any female. A. W. Diamond later (1972) found that in the West Indies the male *Fregata magnificens*, the magnificent frigate bird, ceases to feed the fledgling when it is 3-4 months old, leaves the colony and is not seen again until the ensuing breeding season. The female continues to feed the young bird for a further 3-4 months; this seems to explain the slow development of the fully feathered youngster, and its long hungry wait, and crying out to be fed, at the colony (remarked upon by Nelson), while its harassed mother is at sea searching for enough food to keep herself and her child alive. The desperate young frigate bird eventually learns to find its own food; but mortality is high at this stage. As a result of the prolonged rearing period, the female *magnificens* is unable to breed in the next season; but the male, completing his moult away from the colony, returns in good time to court a new wife and so is able to breed annually. In support of this, Diamond found an excess of female chicks was produced, which must be the case if the male breeds regularly twice, and the female only once, in 2 years.

GANNETS AND BOOBIES

Gannets and boobies have long narrow wings and beaks, streamlined torpedo-shaped bodies and strongly webbed feet, perfectly adapted to long periods of flight, and to spectacular plummet dives from the air upon surface-swimming fish. Usually these dives are shallow, and boobies can take flying fishes at or just above the surface. Gannets dive deepest, but not so deep as has been reported, rarely sinking deeper than 30ft (9·1m), and usually much less. They concentrate on fish they have seen from the air, and which they seize under water in the bill in a normal grasp between both mandibles (they do not spear fish like the anhinga or water-turkey which actually impales the fish and later has some difficulty in extricating its long wedge-shaped bill). Gannets and boobies usually swallow their prey under water—

Brown booby

probably to reduce the risk of air-piracy by frigate bird or skua. They are buoyant, having air sacs around the neck and throat, too buoyant to swim deeper, and they return to try again from the air if the plunge is unsuccessful. Tales of gannets drowned in fishing nets set at 30 fathoms may be true, but without doubt these died as a result of plunging at fish they spotted in the nets as these rose close to the surface—a net may lie for a long time at or near the surface before it is brought aboard. To reach 30 fathoms (180ft) the gannet would take some 90 seconds swimming against increasing pressure at its estimated rate of descent of 2ft per second (the maximum—those expert divers, coot and duck, descend at 1½-2ft per second). Ten seconds would be a long dive for gannet or booby.

There are nine species of these medium-large oceanic birds. Some systematists have placed the cool-water-loving gannets and the tropical boobies in separate genera, but their structure and life histories are so similar that we prefer to regard them as one genus *Sula*, with a tropical origin, doubtless radiating from parent stock in the Pacific, in common with the majority of the vast pelican tribe. While the boobies have proliferated most among the many islands of the warm Pacific and Indian oceans, the three very similar black and white gannets have moved north and south into widely separated breeding grounds. The largest and most successful of these is the North Atlantic *S. bassana* (white tail), so named from its ancient colony on the Bass Rock in the Firth of Forth. The South Atlantic or Cape gannet *capensis* (black tail) is confined mainly to two large colonies off South Africa. The Australian *serrator* (centre tail feathers black, outer ones white) breeds on New Zealand coasts, with small colonies off Tasmania. The gannet's distribution and range are shown in Figure 18.

Conforming to Bergmann's rule that the larger species or subspecies of a genus tend to live in the colder areas of the geographical range, the gannets are almost twice the weight, although not double the size, of the tropical boobies. Of the latter the white booby *S. dactylatra*, closely resembling the true gannets in colour, is the heaviest, and with its all-black tail could be mistaken for the Cape gannet. Incidentally the dense snowy whiteness of these gannets' breasts and backs allows recognition from a considerable distance at sea, distinguishing them from other whitish birds of comparable size, such as the pale-winged gulls. It probably helps the individual to identify and join with other gannets on profitable fishing forays (see page 34), when like most of the boobies they form skeins, as geese do.

Gannets and boobies have no brood patch. They incubate with both feet (all four toes connected by large webs) placed *above* the egg or eggs, the weight of the body

Figure 18 World breeding distribution of the three species of cool water gannet superspecies

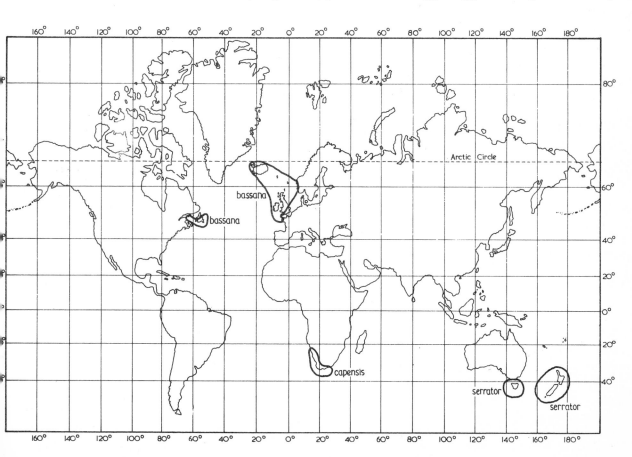

resting on the tarsus. In the broiling heat of the tropical sun they stand *beside* the egg or eggs, careful to place their shadow over them; and the young naked chicks are likewise shadow-cooled in full noon sunlight, although brooded at night and in cool weather.

Display is mutual, as in most birds in which the sexes are outwardly so alike. Usually female boobies are slightly larger and heavier than their mates, but this is reversed in the gannets; and voices are distinctive. The various displays in each species are similar, obviously deriving from a common ancestral source, but yet subtly different. In the boobies there is some aerial display above the colony which is not the case with the gannets. These heavier birds confine their courtship and mating ceremonies strictly to the nest in the crowded gannetry on solid ground.

Gannets occupy their nests early in the spring, the most mature birds arriving first, and one or other of the pair remains in possession until breeding is completed. The reason is obvious: each nest is geometrically sited just beyond the reach of the outstretched bill of a brooding neighbour. If a nest is left unguarded for more than a few minutes neighbours lean across and help themselves to the furniture— seaweed, grass, mud. Also other gannets quickly take possession of a desirable empty centre nest, and the rightful owner will have to fight to regain possession. Finally, gulls and other predators will snatch up egg or young chick if these are left unguarded, as anyone who has disturbed a gannetry will have seen: the nimble predator flies in long before the less agile gannet has circled back and made up its mind to land.

Boobies live in less dense groups, varying from gannet closeness in the guanay booby of Peru, to a space of 50 square yards around each nest in the Abbott's booby, *Sula abbotti*, a rare species which breeds in small colonies scattered widely in the tops of tall trees on Christmas Island, Indian Ocean.

Incubation, by both parents, occupies 41-5 days in the gannets, and rather longer in the boobies (56 days in Abbott's). The single gannet chick grows far more rapidly than the young booby; its food supply of large surface-shoaling fish (eg mackerel, herring, garfish) seems unlimited in summer, so that one or other parent is reliably available to regurgitate as much as the chick desires. In an experiment of placing two chicks in one nest it was proved that one pair of gannets can adequately feed and rear two fledglings. Yet gannets only exceptionally lay two eggs. Ugly, naked and black on hatching, the baby is fed little and often while it is helpless, and brooded until its down has grown sufficiently to insulate it. After 90-100 days in the young gannet (longer in the boobies) the youngster is fully feathered, and usually fatter and heavier than the adult. The fledgling takes off alone, by flopping awkwardly from cliff to sea. It is too heavy to fly, but is able to survive on its fat reserves while it learns to fish and fly as an independent solitary. This is a vulnerable moment in its long life, however, and more than 50 per cent of young gannets die of storm or starvation in their first winter.

The efficient gannets are able to compress their reproduction within the warmer half of the year; this is necessary, since they migrate towards the equator during the rest of the year, and so escape the reduced food supply and poor weather of the winter. The story of the nestling booby is very different. Except for Abbott's and the red-footed species, boobies lay two or three (four in the Peruvian) eggs, but do not necessarily rear more than one chick. Apart from often severe predation by frigate and other birds, breeding success depends on the availability of food, which in turn depends on local weather conditions in tropical and subtropical waters. These can be unreliable, occasionally disastrous. For example, we have described how, if the east-flowing equatorial countercurrent (El Nino) departs from its usual route and pushes the Humboldt Current ten degrees south from the Galapagos, these islands become bathed by warm surface water, diluted with heavy rain, offering little basic planktonic and fish food for the resident sea birds accustomed to forage in the cool Humboldt stream. The fish shoals migrate or perish, and if the birds which feed on them are unable to migrate south, they die in large numbers.

Boobies which have begun to nest when fish are plentiful near home will often cease to visit the breeding ground if they have to go hungry in these circumstances: nest, eggs or young are abandoned. This explains why booby eggs may be laid at any time of year, and why peak layings occur during normal seasonal abundance of surface-shoaling fish. The well-feathered fledgling booby is able to resist an enforced fast better than the downy nestling, but because it often has to fast for several days it grows slowly, at about half the rate of the gannet chick, which is fed as much as it can take daily. Even after it can fly the young booby remains dependent on its parents for two months or more: if food is not forthcoming, it starves.

But why lay more than one egg, if only one chick is reared? Boobies have large feet and can easily incubate several eggs. They will lay again if the first clutch is lost early during the incubation period. The white booby usually lays 2 eggs, about 5 days apart, but the first-born, with the advantage of larger size when the second chick hatches, bullies its smaller sibling and takes all the food if this is limited, so usually the latter soon dies—of ritual fratricide. Better, of course, for one strong chick to be reared than two weaklings. Nevertheless a second egg is a meaningful insurance in case the first is lost during incubation. And in a good season after a bad one, more replacements are reared on the better food supply.

Species	Clutch sizes (eggs)	Incubation period (days)	Fledging period (days)	Post-fledging period (days)	Period between successful breeding cycles (months)
North Atlantic gannet	1	43-44	90	nil	12
South Atlantic gannet	1	43-44	90-100	nil	12
Australian gannet	1	43-44	108	nil	12
Red-foot booby	1	45	130	90+	12+
Abbott's booby	1	56	150-70	80-100	24?
White booby	1-2	43	115	60+	12
Brown booby	1-2	43	105-20	50+	10-12?
Blue-foot booby	1-3	41	102	50+	9-10
Peruvian booby	2-4	42?	100+	40?	12

As the above table shows, the longest period between successful breeding cycles occurs in Abbott's booby, as studied by Nelson on Christmas Island. It lays an exceptionally large single egg, which takes 8 weeks to hatch. It is evidently a far-distant forager, returning to feed the nestling only after long intervals. The youngster grows slowly as a result, and continues to be fed for about 3 months after leaving the nest.

The red-foot has some interesting characteristics. The smallest of the boobies, it is polymorphic (that is with colour forms, white and brown, and intermediates, all freely interbreeding); it lays one egg, usually in a tree-nest which, like that of Abbott's, is spaced well apart from the nearest neighbour. In these two tree-nesters there is no territorial squabbling: there is plenty of room to alight near, instead of, in gannets, only on, the nest. The aggressive gannet greeting ceremony of male stabbing at female in a mixture of fear and friendliness (to discover if she is really his mate), is toned down. Nor is there so much need for the constant mutual billing and preening by which mated gannets relieve the tension of sitting tightly against each other when they meet at the nest. The red-foot sits apart from its mate on a nearby branch, and does not preen her. Each visits the nest chiefly to copulate, or to incubate, brood or feed the chick. But activity lingers later in the evening than with any other booby or gannet, normally heavy night-sleepers. The red-foot is partly nocturnal, with unusually large eyes suited to crepuscular fishing.

On some tropical islands, two or three species of booby may breed near each other, but each keeps to its ecological niche: the semi-nocturnal red-foot builds in trees and bushes; the gannet-like white booby on the barren ground, but sometimes in clearings amid vegetation, usually where it can take off easily into the wind; the blue-foot, most agile on the wing, will nest in a hollow, such as the bowl of a volcanic crater, a windless site from which it takes off vertically with ease—where a gannet would have to scramble out on foot.

The blue-foot, with its long tail acting as an efficient rudder and brake, can make the shallowest dive of all—into 24in of water. Its ability to rear two and even three young in a good season is probably associated with its habit of shallow diving close inshore, which enables it to return with food frequently in the same day. Nelson, observing the blue-foot at the Galapagos, found that the male, smaller than his mate and diving closer inshore, brought small fish often to the chicks, but only in the first half of the period of their dependence on their parents. The female, larger and diving in deeper water, then takes over entirely. She brings home croploads of larger fish, but at longer intervals. The male meanwhile, like the male frigate freed of child-care long before his mate, is able to start displaying again for the next nesting session, within the year. He indulges in his extraordinary ponderous parading walk, handsome bright-blue feet lifted high to advertise himself, and tail cocked. 'Admire me' he seems to say; and if there is no response he will whistle invitingly and leap vertically into the air to circle above the colony, again displaying those bright-blue feet as he returns to earth.

The Peruvian piquero is the most gregarious and prolific of the boobies, breeding in vast numbers (formerly many millions) on the rainless offshore islands of Peru, where along with the guanay cormorants and pelicans it is responsible for the deposits of excreta which have been and are still being exploited at a considerable profit (page 81). The cool Humboldt waters are here so rich in anchovetas that the guano producers do not have to travel far to feed; and none of them is, strictly, an ocean wanderer. The piqueros sometimes darken the sky; on sighting a shoal they will congregate and dive spectacularly en masse. In a normal season the mated pair have no difficulty in raising three chicks, and occasionally four, to maturity. But the piquero needs to rear many replacements to insure against the population crashes which occur periodically when (at intervals of 7 and 12 years in the present century) the warm El Nino moves far south, as already described. The piqueros seem unable to leave their ancestral fishing grounds off Peru, and will die by the thousand in the sterile current.

11 SKUAS, GULLS AND TERNS

SKUAS

For nearly a century the powerful aggressive great skuas, known locally as sea hawks or bonxies, stocky brown, gull-like birds with piratical habits have presented a problem of identification for both field observer and museum taxonomist. Were they one unique bipolar species breeding farthest south in Antarctica as well as on remote North Atlantic islands; wandering in almost every ocean—tropical or freezing cold—of the world during migration and non-breeding periods? You can meet a great skua in the western Mediterranean, off West Africa, Newfoundland, Spitzbergen, Japan, Hawaii, British Columbia, Brazil, and many other places where they do not breed. Sir Edmund Hillary saw one flying over ice and snow only 80 miles from the South Pole; therefore it is considered to be the most southerly bird ever recorded.

There are only four true species of skuas, all breeding in the far north; only one of these also breeds in the southern hemisphere, the great *Catharacta skua*. Its arrival from the north may be a fairly recent event. In its new antarctic and sub-antarctic habitat the great skua is today a successful and expanding superspecies.

Recent field studies and banding results have helped to sort out the distribution of the superspecies into their various forms, and some workers now consider these are valid species. The typical North Atlantic *C. skua* breeds only in Iceland, the Faeroes, and northern Scotland, and probably it numbers less than 3,000 pairs. It has a chestnut tinge to its brown plumage, looks remarkably clumsy, yet is

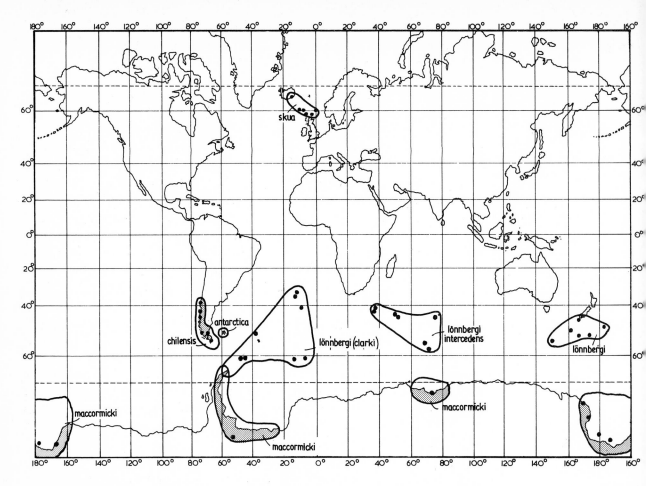

successful in pursuing other birds, forcing them to disgorge the contents of their crop. Although not as nimble and successsful as the frigate bird in catching the vomit, the great skua usually seizes it before or as it strikes the sea. This northern form associates in loose colonies when breeding, and the largest concentrations are at Foula, Unst and Fair Isle in Shetland. Here its main victims are gannets, gulls and terns, and more rarely shearwaters and fulmar petrels. It has been recorded as seizing the tail and upending a flying gannet which failed to disgorge in time. In the absence of other birds fishing at sea, skuas will take surface-swimming fish (they do not normally dive) honestly; they greedily attack carrion such as dead whales, seals and fish, both afloat and ashore. At their breeding grounds they will devour the eggs and young of other birds, rats, lemmings, voles, worms and insects.

This omnivorous appetite and high-seas piracy is likewise typical of the southern forms of the great skua. As shown in Figure 19 the most southerly race is *maccormicki*, confined as a breeder to the south polar continent and its offshore islands. In the non-breeding period this small light-coloured race (no chestnut tinge) wanders north across the equator, reaching India, Japan and Canada, thus conforming to the general concept that the farther south a migrant breeds the farther north it will migrate and vice versa. However it does not fit Bergmann's rule, for it is smaller than the race *lönnbergi* which breeds in the more temperate latitude between 60°S and 30°S, including South Island of New Zealand, South Georgia, Tristan da Cunha and other islands.

Figure 19 Distribution of the superspecies, *Stercorarius (Catharacta) skua*, the great skua. Breeding places embraced by black lines and shaded. Races from both northern and southern hemispheres may cross the equator on migration

The Chilean race *chilensis* inhabits both coasts of South America, and is distinct on account of its warm almost cinnamon tinge, even more vivid than the chestnut of the northern great skua. Finally there is the smallest race *antarctica*, breeding only in the Falklands, like *chilensis* but with a smaller bill; it wanders north to Brazil; despite its small size it is a fearless predator, snatching up the eggs and chicks of other birds, attacking sickly sheep and lambs, and freely striking at human intruders to its nesting ground.

It is still not known exactly how far north these several races of the southern great skua travel when not breeding; certainly they overlap with the wintering zones of the northern great skua. A ringed individual of this species has reached Brazil in March, a month in which some of the Falkland birds would still be present. Hence it is easy to see how individuals of the northern race might have worked south originally, and settled to breed first in south temperate, and at last in antarctic, lands. In time the south polar breeders developed characteristics which made them a race, if not a species, apart. Some of the differences were studied by R. C. Wood at Cape Crozier where 110 breeding pairs of individually marked *maccormicki* nested over eight consecutive seasons. He found that pairs maintain the bond by re-occupying previously established territory. Annual breeding success averaged 0·34 fledglings per pair for 5 years. The northern skuas, perhaps because of their larger breeding and feeding territories, often raise an average of more than one chick. There was a lower rate of success in 36 pairs lacking previous breeding experience, which laid their eggs late, suggesting behavioural difficulties in pair formation. The average survival rate of adults with breeding experience was high, 93·8 per cent for 4 years, sufficient to maintain numbers provided the adults had a breeding span of approximately $15\frac{1}{2}$ years.

The three smaller skuas, the jaegers, present much the same puzzle of identification in the field as the great super-species, at least as far as immatures are concerned. The adult arctic skua (parasitic jaeger) *Stercorarius parasiticus* has a wedge-shaped tail with two long, straight, pointed centre-feathers projecting. These distinguish it from the broad, twisted centre-feathers in the tail of the rather larger, bulkier pomarine *pomarinus*; and from the smallest skua, the long-tailed *longicaudus* with centre-feathers projecting up to 9in beyond the rest of the tail. But as the long tail feathers are not grown in the immatures and are temporarily lost during the adult moult at sea, and all three species have two distinct colour phases, light and dark, identification at sea is difficult. The long-tailed is the most obvious, from its small size, black cap and lack of breast markings—the dark phase is rare in this skua.

All three jaegers are high-arctic in breeding, the long-tailed nesting nearest the Pole, including the inhospitable north coast of Greenland. Some will breed far inland, on the tundra of northern Europe, Asia and Canada, where the ground above the permafrost blossoms into life for three brief summer months, with wild flowers and migrant waders, geese and ducks. And here the jaegers prey much on lemmings which have wintered under the snow, feeding on moss and berries. Breeding success, particularly in the long-tailed skua, is related to the numbers of lemmings it can kill in summer: if lemmings are scarce this skua may fail to breed.

The nesting habits of the skuas are typically gull-like. The male selects a site, and, uttering guttural calls, indulges in a wing-raising display to exhibit the white flashes beneath. A responsive female draws the male to strut around her, making appeasing bowing and head movements which establish recognition. Mutual

Antarctic skuas

excitement ends in bill touching, and occasional aerial flights together. The pair defend vigorously the territory around the nest, a hollow made by the trampling of the ‿ated birds, and lined with grass, moss or peat; on the wet tundra it is raised to form a dry mound. Two dark-brown blotched eggs, the normal clutch, are incubated by both sexes, for the same period as in the larger gulls—27-31 days. To distract ground enemies, such as man, polar bear and arctic fox, there is a realistic injury-feigning act, wings and body trailing and tumbling on the ground as if the bird had become dazed and incapable of flight. As an alternative, the skua will attack from the air, sometimes digging its claws into the intruder and striking repeatedly with wings and beak.

The downy chick seldom remains in the nest longer than 48 hours. It is protectively coloured and skulks near the nest site. If food is scarce the first-born may take all, leaving the other to die of starvation or be pecked to death when it wanders about the colony. At four weeks the young skua is independent; with the approach of their moult the adults lose interest, and it becomes solitary. It may have a lean time bridging the period between desertion and obtaining its first self-gathered meal. It is untrained in piracy, and must pick up a living where it can.

For a year, perhaps two years, the immature skua wanders the ocean feeding-grounds of other sea birds, spending its second summer in warm low latitudes without coming ashore; gradually perfecting its instinctive habit of robbing the other birds by the trial-and-error test. It returns to the region of its birthplace when

2–4 years old, but does not necessarily breed. An arctic skua ringed as a chick in Shetland in July was shot two years later at 70°N in west Greenland on 17 July, hundreds of miles from its birthplace. On return home, young skuas form small clubs or parties outside the breeding group, which have the function of breaking down the isolation of the individual, and of achieving recognition of an eligible mate and suitable breeding site. The usual displays take place, and other gregarious activities include communal bathing in fresh water. At this midsummer time the proportion of nonbreeders can be high. Pryor records that a colony of south polar skuas on Haswell Island, Antarctica, consisted of 23 nesting pairs, and 17 nonbreeders which were ready to take up territories in the same summer.

Some pomarines from the North Atlantic are recorded as crossing the isthmus of Panama, to continue their piratical habits, along with frigate birds, off equatorial coasts of the Pacific and the Humboldt Current. The arctic skua penetrates the Mediterranean, the Red Sea and the Indian Ocean, the Straits of Magellan, and Australasian waters. The long-tailed covers the South Atlantic on its migrations, and both coasts of South America. In the Humbolt Current it chases the piquero boobies in waters where southern great skuas also operate.

GULLS

The large majority of gulls seen at sea are not ocean wanderers. They will follow ships for limited distances of a dozen miles or so from the nearest land, but seldom beyond the continental shelf (100 fathom line). Most of them live within sight of, and roost, on land, or on some sheltered salt or fresh water. Many depend entirely on the land for their food supply. They are a successful group of powerfully built birds which have occupied many of the marine littoral, and some freshwater, niches available to efficient fliers and swimmers. All have webbed feet, swim buoyantly, but seldom dive below the surface.

During the present century, as described in Chapter 4 there has been a considerable increase in those species which have become partly dependent on man, and have taken to scavenging his waste. In the northern hemisphere these flourishing opportunists include many of the *Larus* gulls, especially the herring *L. argentatus*, the great

Black-headed gull

black-backed *L. marinus*, the black-headed *L. ridibundus* and its North American cousin the ring-billed *L. delawarensis*. Their counterparts in the southern hemisphere are the large black-backed (kelp or dominican) *L. dominicanus*; the smaller silver gulls (*L. novaehollandiae, scopulinus, bulleri*); and the brown-headed *L. maculipennis*, and other, more sedentary species. Altogether there are over forty species of gulls, of which some two-thirds belong to the *Larus* supergenus, which has spread over the coasts of the world, evidently from the north, and diversified into many resident species. The only large area of ocean where gulls are absent or do not nest is the tropical South Pacific; but here on the coral atolls and volcanic islands of Polynesia the abundant terns replace them.

Nesting circumpolarly and nearer to Antarctica than any other gull, the powerful kelp *L. dominicanus* may have originated from migrants of the lesser black-back *L. fuscus*, as discussed in Chapter 1. The kelp gull has one of the most extensive breeding ranges of any sea bird, from the antarctic islands north to subtropical coasts of Australasia, South America and South Africa, wherever on these coasts it can exploit a food supply, and particularly at the assemblies of colonial nesting sea birds. Probably it is the world's most abundant gull, yet it is not pelagic in any part of this vast range: except that it moves north from its more polar nesting ground to avoid the long antarctic winter night, it is a resident gull.

Many of the smaller, and a few of the larger, gulls wear brown, black or grey hoods during the breeding season, enhancing their beauty. Other species seem to have worn hoods at one time in their evolutionary history, but now show only traces of them in dark feathers around the eye or nape, when adult; and their immatures may wear distinct hoods only in their first plumage.

The only truly deep-water gull is the kittiwake *Rissa tridactyla*, a small pelagic species, white with pale grey back, black-tipped wings, and dark legs: the juvenile however has the remains of a hood in the black collar at the nape, and has black

Figure 20 (*Left*) Breeding distribution of Sabine's gull, *Xema sabini*. In east Greenland and Spitzbergen it is sporadic; (*right*) breeding distribution of the kittiwake, *Rissa tridactyla*; the black line encloses usual breeding range and black dots represent some known stations. Asterisks mark the three known breeding-stations of *R brevirostris*, the red-legged kittiwake (*after Fisher & Lockley, 1954*)

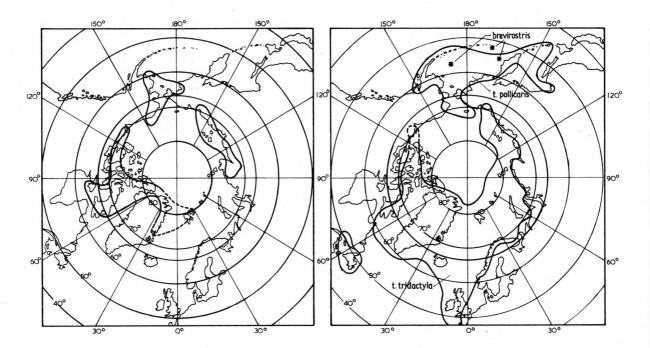

tips to wing and tail feathers. It is a northern cool-water gull, circumpolar in nesting, with a somewhat rare subspecies or species *brevirostris* on some Alaskan islands having red legs and a shorter bill. As Figure 20 shows it shares much of the arctic and boreal area of its breeding range with the fulmar, but in winter ranges farther south than that petrel. It lives with three other hardy gulls breeding in the high Arctic in summer: the pure-white ivory gull *Pagophila eburnea* which often builds its nest on snow- or ice-covered cliffs, and does not migrate far; Sabine's gull *Xema sabini* which in summer has a dark grey hood, forked tail and black wing-tips, an extremely handsome species and a long-distance but strictly coastwise migrant, reaching South America where it is common south to Chile; and the equally handsome rosy or Ross's gull *Rhodostethia rosea*, breeding only in north-eastern Siberia and apparently wintering among the tide cracks and pack ice of the Arctic Ocean (see page 66).

In that great meeting place of sea birds, the Humboldt Current, the arctic Sabine's gull may mingle with the equatorial swallow-tailed gull *Creagrus furcatus*, another hooded species, breeding only in the Galapagos, but making a partial migration south to feed off Peru. It is remarkable for its habit of pursuing its main prey, squid, at night or in the dusk, for which purpose its large dark eye, surrounded with a scarlet orbital ring, is obviously efficient. In doing so, like the blue-footed booby, it reduces the risk of piratical attacks by frigate birds, which sleep heavily at night.

To return to the kittiwake: the adults fly from winter quarters in the wide ocean to their northern nesting sites late in April (a month later in the high Arctic). Ringing has shown that after nesting is completed in August and September, kitti-wakes wander far and wide; those from the polar coasts of Europe tend to seek the open sea around Iceland, southern Greenland and Newfoundland. In the next summer, year-old birds make only a late, half-hearted return towards home, and successful nesting may not take place for another year or two. In mid-winter kittiwakes are seen off West Africa, and in western Mediterranean and nothern Caribbean waters. Usually they appear at sea in small dispersed flocks as they search with graceful buoyant flight, and take food at or near the surface. They are not scavengers, but will follow a ship at times for the sake of the marine organisms churned up by the propellor. Occasionally they will submerge completely in a shallow tern-like dive.

Precipitous cliffs with narrow ledges or projections are preferred, the nest, consisting of grass, moss, seaweed and excreta being built against the sheer rock wall. Kittiwakes in spring form parties which fly to a cliff slope to tear off grass and dirt, which is compacted by the treading movements of the mated pair into a cup sufficient to hold the eggs, usually two. Here the adults spend hours together, side by side, fondling each other with dove-like motions of the bill, and wailing musically, not seldom in duet. A pretty scene, this close and loving contact, with breasts pressed together against the cliff. There is no room for the wing-display of other gulls, but the kittiwake makes up for this with incessant calling, mouth open to display the bright orange-red interior. Just before egg-laying the mutual excitement and calling reach their height; and at last the male places one foot upon the female, pawing her gently. She crouches down, turning her head upwards, mewing in the food-begging attitude typical of the hungry young, and no doubt derived from her experience as a chick. Sometimes the male will stand on her back for several minutes before coition occurs; this seems to be a habit induced by shortage of room on the tiny nest platform.

As in the smaller gulls, incubation takes 21-4 days, both sexes taking part, the male frequently feeding his mate. Despite the constant guard maintained at the nest, the eggs or chicks are often snatched up, and devoured in flight, by determined gulls. The kittiwake will lay again if the first clutch is lost early during incubation; but losses may be higher in late nests because of increased food requirements of predators feeding their young. Although both eggs and chicks are cryptically coloured, the adults are not, and the noisy kittiwake colony attracts the full attention of its enemies.

The chicks, born with eyes open and a thick warm down, are interesting: unlike other baby gulls which actively wander from the nest soon after hatching, they cannot leave the nest safely until they are able to fly. They do not attempt to. When in danger of being blown away in a gale, they cling firmly to the nest with their sharp claws. When, rarely, a kittiwake has built a nest aberrantly on flat ground in a colony of other small gulls or terns, the chicks instinctively remain in the nest cup, and cannot be pushed out of it without undue force. The young are fed by regurgitation, on partly digested marine organisms. Wing-flapping exercises begin on the 30th day, claws gripping the edge of the nest, each chick waiting its turn to perform.

The kittiwake is a successful species and like most gulls is increasing. It has taken to nesting on ledges on tall buildings overlooking salt water in some northern ports.

TERNS OR SEA-SWALLOWS

The oceanic migration of the arctic tern is the classic example, much quoted, of the longest (great circle) distance annually traversed between breeding and wintering grounds, of any bird. *Sterna paradisaea* breeds farthest north of all birds, as far as land extends; and flies south to spend the northern winter in sight of the south polar

Arctic tern

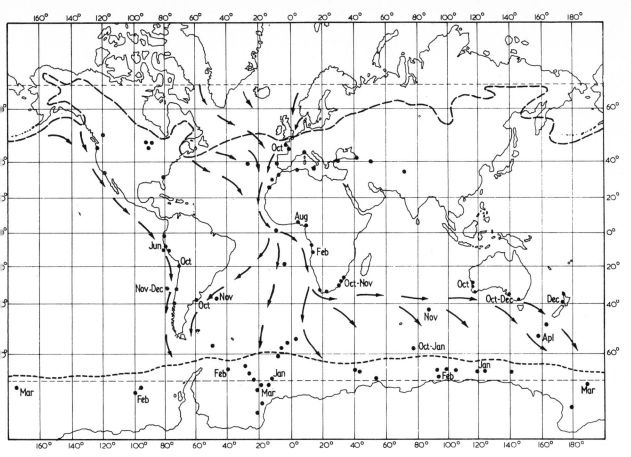

160° 140° 120° 100° 80° 60° 40° 20° 0° 20° 40° 60° 80° 100° 120° 140° 160° 180°

60°
40°
20°
0°
20°
40°
60°

Oct

Aug

Jun
Oct
Nov-Dec
Oct
Feb
Oct-Nov
Nov
Oct
Oct-Dec
Dec
Apl
Oct-Jan

Mar
Feb
Feb
Jan
Mar
Feb
Jan
Mar

160° 140° 120° 100° 80° 60° 40° 20° 0° 20° 40° 60° 80° 100° 120° 140° 160° 180°

Figure 21A Autumn migration and eastward drift towards Australia and New Zealand of the arctic tern, indicated by arrows. Solid circles show records of the species outside of the breeding ground (not complete); the southern limit of the breeding range and the northern limit of Antarctic pack-ice belt are shown by broken lines. (*After Salomousen, 1967*)

ice. Thus it enjoys the maximum amount of daylight, from the midnight sun region of the north to that of the south, with only a few weeks' experience of night darkness during its migration between. A round journey of at least 24,000 miles in the 8 months of the nonbreeding season; making an average of 100 miles a day!

This astounding flight follows two main routes (Figure 21A). The arctic terns breeding in Canada, Greenland, northern Europe and its coasts and arctic islands, and as far east as northern Siberia, converge into the North Atlantic, where prevailing winds carry them east and south toward Africa. The majority pass down the west coast of South Africa in October or early November. Off the Cape of Good Hope they encounter the high winds of the roaring forties, as they head for the antarctic continent, which they reach by a long drifting route on these westerly gales. Those born in north-eastern Siberia, Alaska and the Bering Sea islands move southwards along the whole west coast of America, reaching the fertile waters of the Humboldt Current, where some may winter; but others sweep around Cape Horn and are wind-drifted to Antarctica, along with those individuals which came south via eastern coasts of South America.

Unlike related species of terns, most of which moult during a leisurely and much shorter migration, the arctic tern waits until it reaches the Antarctic before shedding its worn flight feathers. This may be why it hurries through its southward migration, and is seldom observed to feed or rest on the sea while on this journey. It is early summer by the time it arrives at the South Polar pack ice. There is plenty of food available in the abundant euphausian krill of near-freezing water (as in its northern haunts) and the arctic tern settles down to moult and rebuild its fat reserves, depleted during the long migration and fast, amid the penguins, petrels and skuas.

During the austral summer the arctic tern moves closer to the pole as the ice retreats in that direction, and enters a zone of quiet easterly winds complementary to the cyclonic disturbances farther north which helped it to reach Antarctica on its wind-drifted migration. Here, resting much on ice floes, it completes the renewal of its flight feathers. Salomonsen considers that the greatest concentrations of these moulting terns occur in the pack ice between 150°E and 30°W. Thus they do not compete for food with the non-migratory antarctic terns, which they so much resemble that for many decades they were thought to be one species. At this time the resident tern is living near open water, nesting on ice-free dry land of the Scotia and Weddell coasts between 30°W and 80°W. Slightly larger, the antarctic *S. vittata* wears the same bright nuptial dress, black cap, red bill and legs; but by now the arctic tern is clothed in eclipse or winter plumage, with dusky legs and bill, and white forehead.

The coast of the remaining sector, between 80°W and 150°E is virtually devoid of terns in the austral midsummer. It is entered only when the arctic terns begin to go north in March; they are already half way round the antarctic continent from the South Atlantic, and on their spring migration (in the austral autumn) they once more encounter strong prevailing westerly winds in latitudes 60°S to 40°S. Plump and in glossy new plumage, they are wind-drifted north and east. Some strike up the west coast of South America to feed in the Humboldt Current, where

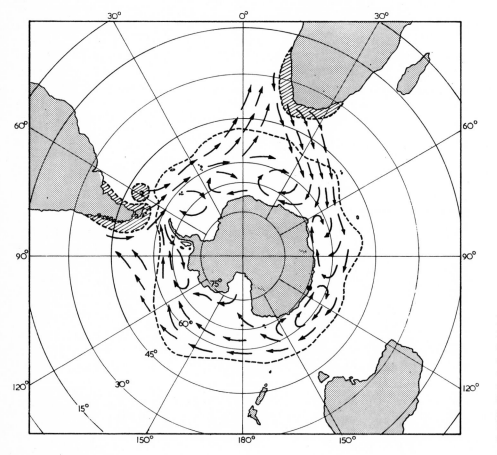

Figure 21B Migratory system indicated by arrows of some arctic terns in the Antarctic, according to Salomousen (1967). Hatched area indicates other winter quarters. Solid circle marks position of recovery of an arctic tern; broken line indicates Antarctic convergence

yearlings may remain the whole summer while the adults continue to their remembered breeding grounds around and north of the Bering Sea. But the majority are wind-drifted through the Drake Passage into the South Atlantic, and northeastwards towards Africa, to feed in the Benguela current, where some juveniles may remain for the (northern) summer, while their parents fly rapidly to their northern European, Canadian and high arctic nesting places. Thus the arctic tern makes a complete circle of the South Polar continent in the austral summer (Figure 21B)—truly an astounding performance for a small bird weighing only a few ounces and with comparatively feeble flight; it is only possible by taking advantage of the global wind system. Unique because no other bird circles the Antarctic in the southern summer, and breeds in the Arctic in the northern summer. Moreover, as already remarked, observation suggests that the migrating adult arctic tern makes most of its voyage along Atlantic or Pacific shores with few feeding or sleeping stops. It is never seen to swim, although it will alight on floating objects, such as driftwood and occasionally the superstructure of a ship. Its normal flight-speed in calm weather must be around 50km (31 miles) per hour; wind-assisted it could be double. If it could fly for 24 hours it could log between 744 and 1,488 miles in one day! Unfortunately we do not know if this is possible. Ringing has shown some mature arctic terns reach South Africa by September, only a few weeks after the completion of the breeding season; and there are many records indicating an average of 100-200 miles a day between date of ringing in the north and recovery in or near South Africa.

The mechanics of continuous flight over several days and nights need no longer surprise us. A few birds seem to be able to fly for weeks, even months, non-stop. (Watching the common swift *Apus apus* over ponds in Devon, I came to the conclusion that this swift normally never touches land during the 9 months of its non-breeding period.) How the arctic tern conserves energy on its long continuous migration is not known, but other terns are noted for their ability to sustain flight for hours on end. In particular the sooty tern *S. fuscata*, nesting abundantly and wandering in all tropical oceans, is never seen to alight on the water. Even when feeding the sooty avoids wetting its feet and feathers, deftly scooping up small fish from the surface. Indeed, it has been shown that the plumage of sooty terns is pervious to water, and that they will drown if confined experimentally in a tank of salt water from which they cannot take flight. Other terns are likewise fastidious about alighting on water: noddy, common, sandwich, black, little and royal make only momentary dives or bill-dipping when feeding. But most terns freely rest on land after feeding, and on flotsam at sea.

None of the terns makes such an extended migration as the arctic, but sandwich, roseate and some common terns are cosmopolitan and catholic in their breeding grounds in temperate and tropical latitudes, and many cross the equator to winter in South America and South Africa.

Most terns are colonial nesters and their colonies, like those of the gulls, are conspicuously noisy. They are capricious and sensitive to disturbance, and will rise into the air simultaneously when a man, dog, fox or other large predator appears. These sudden co-ordinated mass flights, sometimes called 'dreads' or 'panics', are also carried out when no reason is obvious, and may be simply a temporary reassertion of the flocking instinct. Although terns never make a combined attack as the flock hovers above an enemy, the individuals whose nest or chick is threatened will swoop and strike and successfully harry other birds out of the colony, especially predatory heron and gull. Often a tern will defecate accurately upon the intruder during its swoop, and some mammals, especially dogs, retire in discomfort; skunks raiding for eggs or chicks take no notice. Owls and cats take toll by stealth at night. A large ternery is potential feeding ground for many predators, and a mainland site is not seldom abandoned for this reason; royal and sandwich terns are especially prone to change their colony site, even at the egg-laying stage, choosing a fresh place perhaps too late in summer to result in successful hatching and rearing of young (page 51). In general however, terns could not survive if they did not select islands and remote beaches where predation from terrestrial sources is limited.

Their high sociability and habit of placing their nests close together lead to synchronized egg-laying; in arctic and temperate colonies the whole breeding season can be economically completed within 2 months: the incubation period is less than 1 month, and the young terns fly at 4 weeks. But before the egg is laid a few days are occupied with courtship ceremonies, of which fish-carrying is typical. Arriving at the colony with a silvery fish hanging from the bill, the incoming bird calls loudly and is joined by a tern which flies in front, its neck stretched out in contrast with the fish-carrier. The fish is not eaten: it may be exchanged when the pair settle at the nest, newly scraped on the ground, and the other bird may carry it aloft, soon to be joined by its partner; and so the fish-flight is repeated several times, with frequent excited calls. Usually, but not always (the pair may fish together and the female hands the fish to the male in the first place), the male initiates the fish-flight ceremonial, which serves to stimulate both. As in gulls, the male first takes possession of a scrape in the ground, which he advertises by calling, and defends by vigorous pecking. The female tern or gull reveals her sex by a submissive turning away of her head and complacent guttural noises.

The mated female tern (or gull) solicits food from the male by querulous calling and head-jerking, but mated terns will also feed each other. Another difference is that terns feed each other and their young on fresh undigested fish; the gulls regurgitate food. The male noddy has a habit of nodding his head (hence the name?) as he carries a fish and patters near the nest. The female may join him in what has been dubbed the courtship parade; this may end with the female crouching down, and the male then mounts, sometimes standing on her back for several seconds, as if unsure what to do next.

Most terns lay two eggs, occasionally three or four, but more than two chicks are rarely reared. Sooty and noddy terns lay only one egg. Both sexes incubate, changing places often during the day. But in sooty, noddy and bridled terns, where one adult is away feeding for many hours far at sea, the stint may be as long as 24 hours, with nest-relief taking place at dusk or dawn, when the incoming bird may bring home a fish and hand it to its mate.

Terns share the oceans of the world in a nice ecological pattern whereby, even when two or more species nest on the same island, they avoid direct competition for food and territory in various ways: a different food spectrum, and site of breeding, and in the tropics a different breeding season. Thus of both species of noddy nesting on the same islands, as at Ascension and St Helena and in the Bahamas, the brown *Anous stolidus* lays its egg in a stick nest usually on bare rock, but sometimes in bushes or trees, and breeds rather erratically, often twice within 12 months (or more probably two separate groups of brown noddy nest at different times). The black, or white-capped *A. minutus* builds a bracket nest against a rock wall or cliff, and, using the same site each year, develops a substantial platform, well apart from the brown noddy colony both in place and time. It is said to be less pelagic than the brown, but this is doubtful. Noddies are usually seen within 100 miles of land during the nesting season, and do not go hundreds of miles away from it at any time. Yet a curious fact about noddies is that after breeding they seem to vanish completely! Their remarkable sense of orientation and homing ability were proved by Watson and Lashley in classical tests in which individuals returned when released over 850 miles from home.

Common and arctic terns are so alike in the field that where their breeding grounds overlap the cautious observer has been known to record them under 'comic tern' (a fact, not a joke!), unless a clear view of the few distinguishing characters is obtained: the bill is blood-red, the legs shorter, the breast greyer in the arctic tern; the common tern's bill is orange-coloured with a black tip. The calls are similar, but the anxiety note of the arctic is a high whistling 'kee-kee-kee', whereas the common tern adds a grating note ('keeee-yaah!'). Both species feed on small *clupea* fish and some crustaceans near the surface of the sea; and their coexistence at a breeding ground is somewhat uneasy. As discussed in Chapter 3, there is little strife for nest sites between terns, but there are indications of different feeding strategies which have presumably developed as a result of competition. The common tern is dominant in the air, frequently pursuing the arctic which is carrying a *large* fish home to the chicks—evidently the size of the fish triggers off this food parasitism. Burdened with its load the arctic tern is more easily overtaken by the pursuer, who grabs at the fish, often at the awkward moment when the owner stalls and vainly attempts to foil the robber by swallowing it. This pressure in a mixed colony tends to influence the arctic tern to select smaller fish and more crustaceans. The beautiful roseate tern also coexists with some arctic and common terns, but its ecological relationship to the others is not clear. It is proved however that the gregarious terns sometimes fail to rear young at all in a season when fish fry is

Skimmer

scarce; they recruit their numbers in seasons of fish plenty and fine weather by rearing more than one chick per pair.

Marples made tests which showed that common terns have such a strong sense of locality or topographical position that they could alight precisely and dig down to their nest-scrape and eggs when these had been experimentally buried under sand smoothed over to disguise the locality. Also, terns whose nests were moved a considerable distance, by a few feet at a time, returned to brood the eggs after each shift of site; nor were they nonplussed for long after the Marples had altered the appearance of the environment by placing extraneous objects near the nest, and covering it with sand again. Such perception is important to survival, since an extra high tide or storm occasionally provides these hazards, by moving or burying the eggs and altering the contours of the ground and position of local jetsam.

There are many terns which do not migrate far, or at all, and therefore do not come within the scope of this book. There are also terns which migrate, but chiefly by inland or littoral routes, like the black terns of the northern hemisphere.

Most beautiful of all, the fairy tern *Gygis alba* is widespread in tropical latitudes, with subspecies in the Pacific and Atlantic. Its ivory plumage with faint rosy bloom appears transparent against the sunlight, and its dark-ringed eye gives it an ethereal touch. It is equally striking in its choice of a nest site—actually no nest, the single egg being balanced in a slight hollow on a tree branch, where it remains, protected by the adult, even through the tossing caused by sea winds. The chick has strong claws and from birth clings tenaciously to the branch until it is fledged.

The uniquely equipped skimmers or scissorbill terns *Rynchops* have been mentioned. They are long-winged, with odd-shaped bill, the lower mandible much longer than the upper. They feed much by night, the lower bill ploughing the calm surface as the long uplifted wings maintain position. Having stirred the surface with this 'cutwater', the skimmer doubles back on the trail and dextrously snatches up the edible organisms—shrimps and small fish—disturbed by or attracted to the luminescent ripple thus created. Skimmers often associate with other terns in the estuaries of tropical rivers, where they nest during the dry season on the exposed shingle beds.

12 AUKS

Marvellously vivid is the northern summer scene of remote island and precipitous cliff where the vast hosts of the auks assemble and breed, amusing the visitor with their bustling activity, whirring flight, uninhibited calls, ritual gestures, and handsome plumage, against a background of weather-beaten rocks adorned with bright lichens and maritime flowers. The scene is only to be witnessed in the North Atlantic, Pacific and Arctic oceans, for the auks have no family representatives in the southern hemisphere. As already described, by a parallel evolution in both hemispheres of unrelated families of sea birds which live by the pursuit of fish, crustacea and other food under water, the auks occupy the niche in the north which the penguins and diving petrels enjoy in the south. Unrelated, because on the evidence of their structure and palaeontology the auks derive from a common northern ancestor with the gulls and waders, which first appeared in the Eocene epoch, rather later than the first penguins, which have a southern origin. Evidently the main evolution and adaptive radiation of the auks took place in the North Pacific, probably around the Bering Sea, where 16 of the 22 true species still breed, and 12 are endemic. There are only 5 species breeding in the North Atlantic, but 12 nest along the shores of the Arctic, connecting the two main oceans.

Auks are splendid swimmers. They move swiftly under water, beating their half-extended wings like oars, the flight feathers almost closed to form a flexible paddle, the webbed feet trailing as efficient rudders covering the stumpy tail and not used for propulsion except when moving slowly or at the surface. But in the air they are slow and laboured, achieving a normal ground speed of 30-40mph in an undeviating flight; when turning, the webbed feet are spread.

Most of the auks feed offshore but are not often recorded at sea far beyond the continental shelf. Those in the Pacific move south in winter as far as the coasts of Japan and California. In the Atlantic the razorbill *Alca torda* and puffin *Fratercula arctica* make more extensive voyages than the three guillemots (murres) and the little auk. Occasionally puffins are met in mid-North Atlantic; a few individuals marked in the British Isles have crossed to winter on the rich fishing banks off Newfoundland, a resort at that season of immense numbers of the high arctic Brunnich's guillemot (known as the thick-billed murre in America) *Uria lomvia*, and of the large arctic-breeding puffins. On the east side of the Atlantic the southern winter range of razorbill and puffin includes the western Mediterranean and north African coasts; many marked razorbills from the British Isles have been shot in waters off Italy.

Now and then winter 'wrecks' of the little auk or dovekie *Plotus alle* occur on the coasts of western Europe following exceptional cyclones which drive exhausted birds ashore from more northerly wintering grounds. This small hardy auk normally lives all the year within a few hundred miles of the pack ice. Immense numbers breed in Greenland, Jan Mayen, Bear Island, Spitzbergen and Novaya Zemlya, nesting in the frost-shattered debris of arctic cliffs, sometimes far inland.

In the Pacific, little auk and razorbill are unknown. The black guillemot is represented by the crevice-nesting pigeon guillemot *Cepphus columba*; the ledge-nesting *Uria aalge inornata* replaces the Atlantic guillemot, but lacks the latter's variation of a white eye-ring and white line extending back therefrom, which is a character of a varying proportion (nil in the southern to more than 50 per cent in the northern range) of the Atlantic *U. a. aalge*. Puffins in the Pacific are represented by *F. corniculata*, similar to the Atlantic puffin but rather larger and with slightly different bill and facial adornments; and by the distinct large tufted puffin *Lunda cirrhata*, body all brown, face white, long yellow ear-tufts. Finally there are the groups of Pacific auklets and murrelets, filling almost every ecological food and nesting niche in cool northern waters, from Japan in the west along that great arc of island-strewn coast: the Kuriles, the Aleutians, the Bering Sea, Alaska, British Columbia, and south to the Tropic of Cancer at the Gulf of California—that is, to the limit of the cold water of the California Current with its abundant supply of euphausid and small fish food. In this competitive, explosive dispersal the murres took over the ledges on sheer cliffs; the puffins, pigeon-guillemots, murrelets and auklets occupied the holes and crevices in the rocks and dug burrows in the soil, the puffins using the modified claw of the second toe, which is an efficient hoe to rake away spoil hacked out by the powerful bill; the marbled murrelet *Brachyramphus marmoratus* entered sheltered fiords and sought holes in forested slopes; its habits are virtually unknown.

Perhaps most remarkable of all, the Eskimo fog-bird, as Kittlitz's murrelet *Brachyramphus brevirostris* is locally called, is a solitary, laying a protectively coloured egg in the open near the summit of icy coastal mountains in Alaska and Siberia! Did it begin to nest first on mighty sea cliffs thrown up in the last volcanic upheavals many millions of years ago? And move inland to the mountains when auk competitors claimed those seaward precipices? We shall, I fear, never know. But we can admire its adaptive behaviour to nesting in this grim environment of misty mountain and bitter winds. Like the ptarmigan whose habitat it shares, the adult assumes a prenuptial dress that is drab and mottled and hard to see against the background of scree and lichen. How long the young fog-bird remains in the nest, and how it reaches the sea from mountain sites many miles inland, is not known; but presumably it must fly (as the young little auk does from high nunataks inland in Spitzbergen), since to walk so far would involve great danger from its many enemies—bear, wolf, wolverine, fox, falcon, owl and skua. The solitary nesting habit has probably evolved through predation pressures: the farther apart the nests, the less easy is discovery. In winter this hardy murrelet assumes a black and white plumage and haunts the icy waters of glacier-fed seas.

One group of four closely related murrelets are unique in another way: they lay two eggs in a burrow, but instead of nursing the chicks in safety underground the adults chirp and call them down to the sea at night, almost as soon as they are dry from the egg. These chicks have webbed feet almost as large as those of the adult —a nice adaptation to efficient swimming so early in life. Protective colouring is not an advantage in these four murrelets, which are dark above and white below throughout the year, with some slight changes which brighten the head plumage in spring. The legs are long and narrow, the bill inconspicuous. The ancient murrelet *Synthliboramphus antiquus* breeds from the Aleutians to Washington State, its Asian counterpart *S. wumizusume* occupying the same latitude in Japanese waters. Farthest south of all the auks, Xánthus' murrelets breed on small islets along the coast of Lower California; *Endomychura hypoleucos* on the ocean side, *E. craveri* inside the Gulf of California, where the whales come to whelp.

Strange indeed are the lives of the auks, and wonderful is their variety. As yet there is no valid explanation for the pungent odour of citrus fruit given off by the pale-tipped, thick, orange-coloured bill of the crested auklet *Aethia cristatella*. As the black sea-quail (a local name) swim in dense flocks in the Bering Sea you can, as one observer told me, 'smell tangerines half a mile from them!' They are deep divers, collecting euphausid shrimps and fish fry near the sea floor, and storing them in a pouch under the tongue. In the darkness of the burrow the young of crested (also Cassin's and parakeet) auklets sip this food from the parental bill; and remain contentedly at home for over a month, in contrast with the murrelets described above.

Smallest of all the auks, the least auklet *Aethia pusilla* swarms in millions about and north of the Bering Strait. Only 6in long it squeezes into crevices in the crags of Siberian and Alaskan cliffs, where its single white egg is deposited. Incubation is shared in 24 hour shifts, the relief taking place in the dusk of the arctic midsummer midnight. These tiny dark alcids, attractive with their pale eyes and white head plumes, have many diurnal enemies, including Samoyede and Eskimo hunters who net them for food, and must make use of such twilight cover as is available to avoid them. The closely related pygmy or whiskered *A. pygmaea* is slightly larger and in summer sports longer white plumes, some rakishly projecting forward like overlong eyebrows above the crimson bill; it occupies rock crevices southward along the Bering Sea islands. Both these auklets feed on the abundant arctic krill or whalefeed. Still farther south the much larger white-whiskered and eye-browed rhinoceros auklet *Cerorhinca monocerata*, adorned with a curious horn above the bill (hence the name)—all these decorations are moulted in the autumn— behaves more like the true puffin, digging a burrow by night in April on temperate islands south of the Bering Sea, and feeding its chick on raw sand launces and smelt.

The auk's year is divided into three main activities. In the spring there is a sociable assembly which, because auks are most at home on the water, takes place on the sea near the chosen breeding island or cliff. This has been called the loitering ground, where the ritual of courtship, mate recognition or finding a partner, and some copulation, successively occur. Later the paired birds will rest here, preen and wash away the dust of the land; prospecting and nonbreeding individuals will join them when the second period, four months devoted to incubation and rearing ashore, is well advanced. The rest of the year, the autumn and winter, is the pelagic period, during which the wing quills are moulted, and for a while all auks are flightless.

The breeding habits of the ledge-nesting guillemots or murres (*Uria* spp) form an interesting contrast with those of the burrow- or crevice-nesting puffins and the majority of the auklets. Nesting communally, many pairs side by side filling cliff ledges often so narrow that the individual cannot rest full-length on its egg, the guillemots have evolved a pattern of behaviour which ensures survival in the many apparent hazards of such a precarious site. L. M. Tuck estimated that there were at least 56 million ledge-nesting murres in the world, in the proportion of three of the thick-billed or arctic murre *U. lomvia* to one of the common guillemot *U. aalge*. Investigating the reasons for their coexistence where the two species nest together on cliffs in the low-arctic and boreal common boundary of their breeding range, L. Spring found anatomical differences which seem to explain it. The common guillemot has a more upright walk and can dominate the more shuffling thick-bill, forcing it to occupy the narrower ledges. It is also a more agile swimmer, pursuing pelagic fishes near the surface. The thickbilled murre has longer wings and a stouter body, making it more powerful, pressure-resistant and stable in diving for and exploiting the fish and invertebrates on the sea floor of its cooler, more arctic range.

This is a general pattern for co-existence in the auks, this sharing of the food spectrum of the layers of the sea, with their different temperatures, prey (or ages of prey) species. Other auks which exploit the lower, benthic, zone are the black *Cepphus* guillemots—the tystie *C. grylle* of the north Atlantic and Arctic, and its Pacific cousin the pigeon guillemot *C. columba*, which has a considerable longitudinal breeding range from the Bering Sea south to the famous scenic cave on the Santa Cruz Isles, California—where it lays its two eggs in grotto crannies.

As in all birds breeding in dense colonies, the mature experienced adult is first to return to the familiar nest site, to secure and guard it. On mild, usually calm, days in the southern part of its range in the Atlantic and Pacific, the common guillemot or murre pays visits (so does the hole-nesting Cassin's auklet of California and Oregon) as early as Midwinter Day, and more freely during January and February, at least three months before the egg appears. This is most noticeable at very large colonies of several thousand pairs, where competition for nesting space is severe. The preliminary visits usually take place early in the morning: the main flight will assemble at dawn on the sea beneath the cliffs.

After ceremonial 'recognition' dances, skatings and divings, which are really displacement activities or letting off steam, and accompanied by groaning noises, the common murres begin leaving the water and flying up to occupy the ledges, by now washed clean of the excreta of last summer by winter storms. The guttural conversation breaks out afresh among those pushing, bill-waving and jostling for position. As more arrivals flutter clumsily to land they may accidentally bump,

In the high latitude of northern Norway, the range of the arctic (Brunnich's) guillemot with white line on bill overlaps that of the southern guillemot with plain bill

and tumble off the ledges, those already in possession. By noon the visitation is over. It may not be repeated for several days, depending on the weather and most probably on the local availability of this murre's seasonal fish food. In the early spring the supply inshore seems to be irregular.

Razorbills are a little later in reaching the loitering ground in spring; and puffins do not appear until late March in the southern breeding grounds (a month later in the Arctic). Both retreat at intervals, to feed in the open sea.

All three lay their single egg in May, the puffin sometimes in late April. But while the puffin has ample room and privacy in its burrow, and the razorbill a little less in its crevice, the guillemot on its ledge is cheek-by-jowl with its neighbour. Even when, as in many southern colonies (sadly) today, guillemots are rapidly decreasing in numbers, their innate gregariousness is such that they maintain the same density per square foot by moving towards the centre of population, abandoning the outer site (see page 50). It is doubtful if a single pair of cliff guillemots could breed successfully out of sight or hearing of other breeding pairs; I have never seen it. They seem to need the stimulation of the crowd, despite the argument and jostling which the slum-like conditions create. The guillemot avoids the savage territoriality shown by the gannet, whose nest is a substantial structure spaced just far enough apart for one sitting bird to be unable to strike the next. Instead it maintains its territorial integrity by loud intimidating squawks and vigorous waving of elevated bill. Sparring is rare among neighbours; only when a strange guillemot attempts to land beside a brooding bird does the latter stab it, usually toppling the intruder over the edge.

There are other interesting adaptations to ensure breeding success in the crowded loomery, where the eggs and chicks attract gulls, ravens and other predators. One adult remains permanently on guard, but if by mischance or death both parents are absent, it is likely that an unoccupied adult—of which there always seem to be a number available in a large loomery—will waddle forward and eagerly push the egg under its brood spot (emperor penguins will pirate an unguarded egg in this way—incidentally preventing the embryo chilling to death). R. A. Johnson believes that the guillemot can recognise its own egg, since each egg is distinctive with its own pattern of colour and markings, and endeavours to shuffle it to its old position, if it has rolled or been moved along the ledge. He also records a guillemot 'stealing' an egg, covered with mire, from a depression (in wet stormy weather some eggs are blown into crevices and may become irretrievably stuck there in faeces and mud), and moving it some twelve feet to its own territory.

Humans collect eggs from some sites for food, and many are also lost through the visits of birdwatchers and sightseers: in taking flight suddenly, the frightened adults are not always able to disengage the large egg from the brood spot between the legs in time to leave it in a safe position on the narrow ledge. Even if the unguarded egg does not topple into the sea it may be snatched by gull or other predator. Visitors to sea-bird sanctuaries ought not to approach too close to guillemot colonies.

The handsome large egg is incubated with the large end tucked into the cavity of bare skin below the breast, the webbed feet being shuffled partly under the egg to steady and support it. However, there is so much natural disturbance of coming and going, gesticulation and shuffling, between mated pairs, neighbours and insistent visitors, that the much coveted egg is moved about a lot, and often partly exposed to the cool sea air. It is a matter of surprise to me that there should be good hatching success in the circumstances! A guillemot colony is however, comparatively peaceful by night, as the majority of adults enjoy interludes of sleep while incubation proceeds.

Ledge-nesting auks will lay a second egg if the first is lost soon after laying. The black and pigeon guillemots, ancient and Xánthus' murrelets, comparatively safe in their holes under rocks and boulders, have two brood spots and lay two eggs, and yet it is not often that black guillemots rear two chicks. One of the eggs appears to be deliberately neglected and gradually pushed aside. As in some boobies, two eggs may be a form of insurance, but this auk does seem to be evolving towards a one-egg clutch. Other auks with two brood spots have already done so: the razorbill, puffin and Cassin's auklet incubate their single egg, lopsidedly, by leaning upon it with one wing drooped, the egg warmed against the rather inadequate patch of bare skin on one or other side of the lower breast. It is probable that the puffin once laid two protectively coloured eggs in a more open situation like that of the razorbill, which produces one large cryptically marked and coloured egg. The puffin's egg, new laid, appears to be pure white (as most hole-nesting birds' eggs are; white is most easily seen in the semi-darkness) but if held up to the light, well-defined markings of pale brown and lilac can be detected beneath the chalky surface. It may also be significant that these species (also the little auk), with two brood spots occasionally lay two eggs, but never rear more than one chick. In its heyday the great auk, like the cliff-nesting guillemots, incubated its large handsomely marked egg in a central brood spot beneath the breast, the best position for a species which, as we know from the accounts of the slaughter of the vast colony on Funk Island, Newfoundland, crowded as closely together as the common guillemot does.

Hatching a large egg on the bare rock of narrow cliff ledges may seem an inefficient business; yet in the past at least it has worked. Arctic guillemots are extremely abundant; it is only of late that the southern or boreal races have declined, as already discussed in Chapter 6, as a result of man's pollution of the marine environment. Guillemots evolved as open-site cliff-breeders almost certainly as a result of competition among ancestors nesting in less precarious situations; and in the process those chicks which left the dangerous ledges earliest for the safety of the sea were the most successful. This has resulted in the early period of dependence of the chick on the land being reduced to a minimum in the cliff-nesting guillemots and razorbill, as shown in the accompanying table.

| Open-site breeders | Average period in days | | |
	Incubation	Fledging	Total
Common guillemot	33	16	49
Arctic guillemot	30	16	46
Razorbill	34	16	50
Hole-nesting			
Black guillemots	30	40	70
Cassin's auklet	37	45	82
Puffin species	40	45	85

Young guillemots and razorbills are in fact less than half grown when they leave the cliffs. As their primaries are not developed, they descend to the sea by beating the air with their wing covert feathers. Calling excitedly, they flutter rather than fly downwards to the water, generally in the evening when there is less likelihood of attack by predatory gulls and skuas. Although thus early fledged from the land, they are attended by one or both of the parents, who have responded to the piping call of the chick even before it reached the water, and immediately guard and convoy it, and feed it at sea. Adult and young swim rapidly away from the land. If attacked from the air by predators, adult and young dive together and escape by swimming some distance under water.

There is good evidence that the cliff-hatched guillemot chick is sometimes adopted by adults other than its parents: I have seen one chick brooded by three different adults in the course of several hours of observation, during which the chick moved restlessly about the ledge. Promiscuous or co-operative child care in birds is rare, but has been recorded in arctic tern, penguin and moorhen, as well as in several passerines (eg swallows, bee-eaters and the *mohoua* warblers of New Zealand; in the last two females sometimes combine to incubate and feed progeny in the same nest). But this 'helping' does not occur in the razorbill, which although a cliff-nester more often rears its chick in a safer, more private part of a guillemot

Little auks nest in frost-shattered debris of arctic shores beyond the limit of permanent human habitation

ledge, frequently under cover of a slab of rock; nevertheless its chick remains only for the same brief period on land.

Contrast this behaviour with that of the hole- and burrow-nesting activities of puffins, black guillemots, several auklets and little auks. Safe under cover, the chick has no urgent need to get to the sea. It is fed on small raw fishes (also crustacean plankton in the little auk and most of the Pacific auklets) and, over the much longer period ashore, becomes as large as the adult before leaving for the sea. It is then very fat; and like the shearwater, petrel and gannet, is deserted, and remains fasting under cover for a few days while exercising its wings before departure. Not that there is much room to exercise in crevice or hole, but, for a short period in the last night or two, it will come forth and flap its wings, returning to cover before dawn. Even so, its take-off down to the sea is a scrambling walk rather than sustained flight, although a high wind may assist it to become airborne and lift it clear to sea. The fledgling little auk, which may be hatched in a cliff crevice far inland in the Arctic, can fly well enough to reach the sea, although some fall by the way, and in scrambling to the nearest vantage point for another take off they are in danger of being taken by arctic fox, falcon, snowy owl, skua or gull which haunt the vast loomeries at this season.

From the evidence of banding young auks it is known that few are mature enough to breed successfully until they are two years old—even three and occasionally four years old in the larger species. This is clear to the observer visiting the auk colonies about the time the eggs are hatching. The ledges, rocks, cliff-slopes and loitering ground on the sea below contain far more adults than in the spring mating period, and many of these are new arrivals in fresh-looking plumage unabraded by contact with the land. They are the adolescents, preparing for the future by familiarising themselves with the terrain. They make short excursions ashore, and sit about, idly conversing and displaying, meeting future partners but not copulating, temporarily occupying available space in or at the edge of the colony.

The breeding adults tolerate these visitors so long as they do not trespass too close. It would be pleasant to believe that an immature auk, returning to the actual place where it was hatched, would be recognised and accepted by its parent. But this is unlikely: its adult plumage and voice would be different from these characters by which its parents last identified it at the parting at fledging time at sea in the autumn of yesteryear. Marking of young auks has shown us only that many individuals return to breed at or near the site where they were born, but some turn up to pair with strangers at colonies farther afield, and so add fresh blood to maintain the vigour of the species within the geographical range, and common heredity.

The eggs, flesh and feathers of the auks have been important in the economy of northern peoples since time immemorial. In some remote arctic regions they still are. In the spring the fresh eggs were collected, especially those of the guillemots along all coasts from California and Japan to the Arctic, and from Portugal and Maine to Greenland and Novaya Zemlya. At the last place they are, I believe, still 'farmed', by taking only a proportion of the first laying. Guillemots will lay a second egg, occasionally a third, if the first (or second) is taken as soon as laid. During the late nineteenth century, some half-million murre eggs, collected from the offshore islands of California, were sold each spring in San Francisco, fetching up to 20 cents a dozen. 'Egging' the steep cliffs of Flamborough Head in Yorkshire was a traditional custom, men with baskets descending on ropes to collect gull, guillemot and razorbill eggs by the thousand for a short period in May. The practice is discontinued since protection was afforded the auks, now greatly decreased in numbers. But in the Faeroes, Iceland, and all Eskimo and Arctic coast lands it continues.

The adult and fledgling auks were (and are) taken in long nets laid beneath the auk rookeries; or by a special hand net (the Icelandic *fleygustong*) wielded, as in the game of lacrosse, by a hunter crouched on cliff or shore where the auks fly past on the updrafts of air; or with a hair noose at the end of a long rod, patiently, skilfully, flipped over the head of a resting bird. For banding purposes I have caught many puffins, razorbills and guillemots with a wire crook at the end of a long bamboo rod, pushed slowly forward until the flattened hook could be slipped over the flat tarsus—it is astonishing that these birds, watching the approach of the rod with apparently complacent curiosity, do not connect it with danger, and often auk bystanders do not take flight when the captured bird is drawn away, fluttering and growling protest.

Auks were preserved for winter consumption by plucking or skinning, then wind-drying, smoke-curing or salting the flesh. Eskimo people used to fill a skin, taken whole from a seal with the subcutaneous blubber lining still attached, with the bodies of auks, chiefly little auks, and cache it in a cool place. (The Danish explorer Peter Freuchen tells the story of an aged Eskimo grandmother who, because her usefulness to her tribe had ceased with her failing strength, was abandoned by the wayside during a hunting migration at the end of summer. At that time it was accepted that old unfit persons must not burden the family and hinder its seasonal movements; and the old lady toddled away into the snow, philosophically resigned to die of cold and hunger. Crawling into a cave in the rocks, she discovered a hunter's cache in the form of a large sealskin packed with auks in jellified blubber, a delicious meal which lasted her the whole winter. She emerged in sound condition in the spring to surprise her tribe, on their returning migration, and live another summer of plenty with her people.)

13 PHALAROPES

Many species of land birds have been seen occasionally hundreds of miles at sea. If, as often happens, any of these come aboard ship and remain for a while, it is usually because they are exhausted and blown off course on a normal migration. Included in these visitors are a number of northern wading birds which make considerable trans-ocean journeys; but if in sound condition they will fly past ships, rather than alight. These thin-necked long-legged travellers are quite good swimmers, but never feed and rarely rest on the open sea. On their migrations some make regular stops at traditional places along the route: at islands and headlands where they rest and feed, chiefly by wading and probing along the shore. But the innate impulse to migrate is powerful only during a limited period of days, and so long as the bird has adequate fat reserves to provide the fuel to keep its wings beating it will continue to fly onwards to winter quarters, with little or no dawdling.

On arrival the migratory wader settles down to moult and feed by shore, marsh, lake or other winter habitat in the southern hemisphere, spending at least half the year enjoying its 'winter' in the warmth of the southern summer. Some immature waders will remain longer in winter quarters in the more temperate and sub-tropical southern latitudes; with gonads undeveloped they lack the sexual stimulus to return to the nesting grounds until they are approaching two years old.

The phalaropes are exceptional in that when not breeding they are truly oceanic. They are unique among waders in having partially webbed or lobed feet, probably adapted to their normal habit of paddling and pirouetting on the surface when feeding at sea in winter, and on pond and lake in their arctic breeding grounds in summer. This habit of rapidly spinning (two-thirds of individuals spin to the right) while floating buoyantly on the water serves the purpose of stirring and bringing invertebrates and other food to the surface. The action is accompanied by frequent side-to-side dabbing of the bill; at other moments the phalarope zig-zags forward, head bobbing and bill snapping up food. It will also upend, and sometimes dive briefly. The plumage is thicker than in other waders, with a close down beneath, obviously an adaptation for waterproofing.

At sea huge flocks of phalaropes are sometimes encountered, feeding in suitable zones, especially amid floating seaweed. When so occupied they are extremely tame, and easily approached to within a few yards. In flight they move erratically, with sudden twisting changes of direction. This, and their small size, has earned them the name of sea-snipe. A flock will wheel in close formation, then settle with a steep swoop upon the water.

The phalaropes are further unique in the female being more brightly coloured than the male, and she has no brood patch. Instead the cock, literally henpecked, is courted by the female, who displays at and may mate with several males during the breeding season. After flirtation and mating (often on the water), she encourages the male chosen as her immediate consort to visit suitable nest-sites, of which several may be made by breast-rotating in long grass near the water's edge. She lays four pear-shaped, protectively coloured eggs in one of these, and a day or two later abandons the nest. The cock assumes all family cares, having developed a large bare breast patch for incubating the eggs. Quite alone he hatches these; and nurses and protects the downy chicks until they are independent at 3 weeks old.

If the eggs or chicks are threatened by the approach of a predator, the father phalarope throws himself in its path, screaming to attract attention, and realistically feigning injury. Tumbling and staggering along with apparently broken wings and legs, always just out of reach, he lures the intruder far away from the nest. The cryptically coloured young meanwhile have 'frozen' to the ground at his first signal of alarm.

The whole business of courtship, nidification and rearing is completed in some six weeks of the brief arctic summer. Of the three species, two have nearly identical habits: the northern or grey *Phalaropus fulicarius* and the red-necked *P. lobatus* both nest by ponds and lakes on the tundra or seashore, circumpolarly. The female lays her eggs late in June, and migrates in July. The males and young leave during August. Both cross the equator to winter in all oceans as far as the southern limits of Asia, America and Africa, including the coasts of Arabia, the Philippines and even occasionally New Zealand (Figure 22). The cool waters of the Humboldt and Benguela currents are favourite feeding grounds in the austral summer, where the dainty phalaropes mingle with pelicans, boobies, gannets, penguins, shearwaters and petrels, pirouetting and dabbling after planktonic food ignored by the larger birds. Fragile-looking as the smallest storm petrels, the phalaropes ride gales at sea with the same skill; but swim much, and, as we have seen, normally enjoy the best weather in their world by living in summer for most of the year.

The third phalarope, Wilson's *Steganopus tricolor*, nesting in central and western North America, is much less maritime, lacks the scalloped toe lobes, is more of a wader, and frequents estuaries and inland lakes on migration south to Chile and the Argentine.

Waders are related to the great order of skuas, gulls, terns and auks, which evidently evolved in the northern hemisphere, where the majority breed. But as in

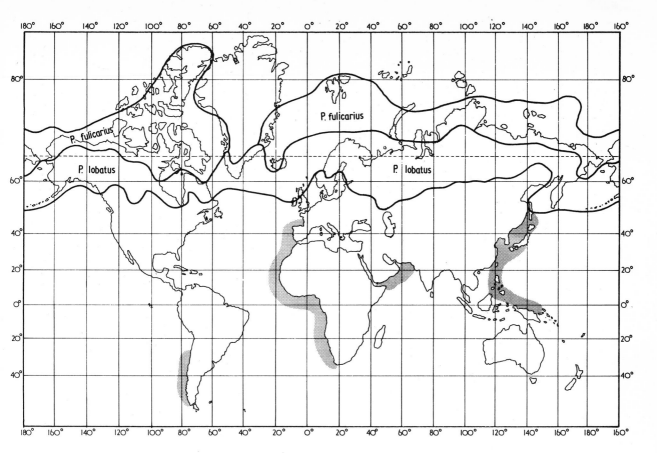

Figure 22 The breeding grounds (within thick lines) of the two *Phalaropes* overlap. The wintering grounds are stippled. The grey *P fulicarius* is more marine all the year than the red-necked

certain skuas, gulls and terns, a few of the waders now breed far south of the equator. Most of these southern-breeding waders are sedentary, but have closely specific relatives in the north, indicating clearly their ancestral source. A few have developed into distinct genera: for example the curious wrybill *Anarhynchus frontalis*, as large as a sparrow, a kind of plover but unique because its bill turns to the right asymmetrically—an adaptation to seeking food under stones. It is only found in New Zealand, breeds in mountain river beds, and winters along the shore; total numbers, about 6,000.

Some trans-ocean waders	Oceans visited		
	Pacific	Atlantic	Indian
Grey plover *Pluvialis squatarola*	R	R	R
Golden plover *Pluvialis dominica*	R	R	R
Curlew *Numenius arquata*		R	R
Long-billed curlew *Numenius madagascariensis*	R		
Bristle-thighed Curlew *Numenius tahitiensis*	R		
Whimbrel *Numenius phaeopus*	R	R	R
Bar-tailed godwit *Limosa lapponica*	R	R	R
Black-tailed godwit *Limosa limosa*	R	R	R
Greenshank *Tringa nebularia*	west only	east only	R
Wandering tattler *Tringa incana*	R		
Common sandpiper *Tringa hypoleucos*	west only	R	R
Terek sandpiper *Xenus cinereus*	west only	R	R
Turnstone *Arenaria interpres*	R	R	R
Knot *Calidris canutus*	R	R	rare

Species			
Dunlin *Calidris alpina*		R	R
Pectoral sandpiper *Calidris melanotos*	R	R	
Curlew sandpiper *Calidris ferruginea*	rear east	R	R
Little stint *Calidris minuta*		R	R
Red-necked stint *Calidris ruficollis*	R		
Purple sandpiper *Calidris maritima*	north only	north only	
Sanderling *Calidris alba*	R	R	R
Broad-billed sandpiper *Limicola falcinellus*	R	R	R
Ringed plover *Charadrius hiaticula*	east only	R	

Notes: R = regular in that ocean. The above are species only; there are valid or doubtful subspecies or races in most migrant waders.

BIBLIOGRAPHY

This is not a complete list of works consulted while preparing this book—that would have occupied perhaps fifty pages and greatly added to its cost. For this reason I give only the authorities mentioned in the text, but have added a few on sea birds which have deservedly become classics. Long titles to some scientific papers have been shortened.

Alexander, W. B. *Birds of the ocean* (1955)

Armstrong, E. A. *Bird display and behaviour* (1947)

Buxton J. & R. M. Lockley, *Island of Skomer* (1950)

Darling, F. F. *Bird flocks and the breeding cycle* (1938)

Diamond, A. W. 'Sexual dimorphism and unequal sex ratio in frigate birds', *Ibis* 114: 395 (1972)

Falla, R. A. Papers on sea birds in the south-west Pacific, 1934-70

Fisher, H. I. 'Experiments in homing in Laysan albatrosses', *Condor* 73: 389 (1971)

Fisher, H. I. 'Sympatry of Laysan and black-footed albatrosses', *Auk* 89: 381 (1972)

Fisher, H. I. & M. L. Fisher. 'Visits of Laysan albatrosses to the breeding colony', *Micronesia* 5: 173 (1969)

Fisher, J. *The Fulmar* (1952)

Fisher, J. & R. M. Lockley. *Sea birds* (1954)

Fleet, R. R. 'Red-tailed tropic bird on Kure Atoll', *Auk* 89: 651 (1972)

Gurney, J. H. *The gannet* (1913)

Hardy, A. C. *The open sea* (2 vols) (1956 & 1959)

Harris, M. P. 'Biology of the dark-rumped petrel', *Condor* 72: 76 (1970)

John, D. D. 'The second antarctic commission of R.R.S. *Discovery II*', *Geog Journ* 83: 381 (1934)

Johnson, R. A. 'Nesting behaviour of the Atlantic murre', *Auk* 58: 153 (1941)

Kepler, C. B. 'Polynesian rat predation on Laysan albatrosses', *Auk* 84: 426 (1967)

King, W. B. *US Wildlife Serv SS Rep Fish* 586: 1 (1970)

Kooyman, G. L. *et al.* 'Diving behaviour of emperor penguin', *Auk* 88: 775 (1971)

Lack, D. Papers and books on territory, ecology, speciation, population, 1934-71

Lawrence, G. N. *Proc US Nat Mus* 1: 48 (1898)

Lockley, R. M. Papers and books on sea birds, including *Shearwaters* (1942); *Puffins* (1953); *Animal navigation* (1967); 'Non-stop flight and migration in the common swift', *Ostrich* suppl 8: 265 (1970)

Lockley, R. M. & S. Marchant. 'A midsummer visit to Rockall', *Brit Birds* 44: 373 (1951)

Marples, G. & A. Marples. *Sea terns or sea swallows* (1934)

Matthews, L. H. 'The birds of South Georgia', *Discovery Rep* 1: 561 (1929)

Mayr, E. *Systematics and the origin of species* (1942)

Murply, R. C. *The oceanic birds of South America* (1936)

Murply, R. C. 'New light on the cahow', *Auk* 68: 266 (1951)

Nelson, B. *Galapagos: islands of birds* (1968)

Nelson, B. 'The biology of Abbott's booby', *Ibis* 113:429 (1971)

Pryor, M. E. 'The avifauna of Haswell Island', *Antarct Res Series* 12:57 (1968)

Rice, D. W. & K. W. Kenyon. 'Breeding cycles of Laysan and blackfoot albatrosses', *Auk* 79:517 (1962)

Richdale, L. E. Publications on penguins and petrels breeding in New Zealand area, 1939-64

Roberts, B. B. 'The life cycle of Wilson's petrel', *Brit Graham Land Exp Sci Rep* 1:141 (1940)

Salomonsen, F. 'Geographical variation of the fulmar', *Auk* 82:327 (1965)

Salomonsen, F. 'Migratory movements of the arctic tern', *Biol Medd Dan Viv Selsk* 24:1 (1967)

Salomonsen, F. 'Birds useful to man in Greenland', *Proc IUCN Alberta* 19:169 (1970)

Serventy, D. L. 'Ecology of the short-tailed shearwater', *Proc IOC* 14:165 (1967)

Snow, D. W. & B. K. Snow. 'Breeding season of Madeiran petrel in the Galapagos', *Ibis* 108:283 (1966)

Sparks, J. & T. Soper. *Penguins* (1967)

Spring, L. 'Adaptations in common and thick-billed murres', *Condor* 73:1 (1971)

Stonehouse, B. *Wideawake Island* (1960)

Sverdrup, H. V. *et al. The Oceans etc* (1942)

Thomson, A. L. *et al. A new dictionary of birds* (1964)

Tickell, W. L. N. 'The dove prion', *Falkland Is Dep Surv Sci Rep* 33 (1962)

Tickell, W. L. N. 'Breeding frequency in two albatrosses', *Nature* 213:315 (1967)

Tickell, W. L. N. 'Biology of the great albatrosses', *Antarctic Res Ser* 12:1 (1968)

Tuck, L. M. *The murres* (1960)

Warham, J. Papers on petrels and penguins of Australasia, 1955-72

Watson, J. B. & K. S. Lashley. 'An historical and experimental study of homing', *Pap Dep Marine Biol Carnegie Inst Washington* 7:9 (1915)

Westerskov, K. 'Ecological factors affecting nesting royal albatrosses', *Proc IOC* 13:795 (1963)

Wilson, E. A. MS notebooks on ornithological work in Antarctic, 1901-3

Wingate, D. B. 'Discovery of black-capped petrels in Hispaniola', *Auk* 81:147 (1964)

Wood, R. C. 'Population dynamics of south polar skua', *Auk* 88:805 (1971)

INDEX
Sea Birds and Sites